Angels walk beside you

LILA LOTUS

DEDICATION

This book is dedicated to my angelic guides, and archangel Gabriel, who steered me to this celestial world. To my parents Nestor and Teresa, my son Gabriel, my husband Jack, and all those who wish to change our planet. For my daddy Nestor, please accept this gift for your first birthday in Heaven.

.

CONTENTS

ACKNOWLEDGMENTS

My appreciation begins with the Great Spirit, the Father and Mother Creator of everything. For the magnificent design my soul guides have chosen for me in this life. These experiences have allowed me to grow and have entrusted me with great knowledge and wisdom.

To my parents, Nestor and Teresa. You were the channels that allowed me to manifest my dreams. You have been the most amazing teachers in my life. You have been great coaches and have guided me exactly where my soul needed to go. I am blessed to continue have you in my life: my Father in Heaven guiding my spiritual adventure; and my Mother holding my hand in the womb of Pachamama.

To my ancestors, all of those who have walked before me. Today you have transcended and your legacy which lives within me. Thank you for our encounters and all your messages you have and continue to entrust in me.

To my two sisters Tania and Tatiana, my 49 cousins, my aunts, my uncles, my family in Bolivia expanded in Japan, USA, Spain, and Germany. Thank you for all the celebrations we share as a tribe. These are cherished memories for me.

To my husband Jack, my love and life partner. Because behind any 'Mother' spiritual worker, there is a great man covering all the daily stuff so we can continue evolving as a family. Thank you, my love, for covering me while I give classes, workshops, and retreats. Thank you for taking care of our son with love and patience.

To my son Gabriel, for teaching me pure unconditional love. For being a master teacher for lessons I've never imagined. Thank you for your life and allowing me to create life. You are a miracle of God, a miracle of the angels. So, for that, always honor your life.

To my teachers and mentors, who have guided me at the right time, and in the right order along the way. Thank you for your patience, your love and dedication. For you, I am here today.

To my students, for those who followed the teachings of the angels since the beginning when I started. Thank you, Carmen Garzon, for encouraging me to use my gifts to create the angel classes, helping me on this journey of sharing angelic messages.

To my dear friends who believed in this book. Thanks Carmen Liliana Mejia, for all the beautiful drawings. For your love and dedication to the angels. To Malgorzata Biardzki, Deedre Tanski Morales, Michelle Gausman, Carola Novoa, Jeanette Garcia Blanco, and Claudia Zapata you are my doula angels for this book.

To my dear archangel Gabriel, the first one who revealed himself to me in my Paris apartment 17 years ago. Thank you for coming again and again and holding my hand, guiding me to this amazing world of the angels. You persist and exist with me in every moment. This is for you, my eternal friend. Thank you for introducing me to all the other angels, ascended masters, sacred plants, and spirits of nature. Thank you for the miracle in my womb, thank you for my son Gabriel. He couldn't have another name. This is my honor to you dear celestial friend.

To archangels Ariel, Azrael, Chamuel, Haniel, Jeremiel, Jophiel, Metatron, Michael, Raguel, Raphael, Raziel, Sandalphon, Uriel and Zadkiel for all your teachings and support. To Jesus, the ascended masters, the sacred plants, San Pedro, and spirits of Nature for all the ancestral wisdom shared with me. You live in my soul!

MY RELATIONSHIPS WITH ANGELS

I believe that everyone is connected to angels and spiritual guides from the time that they arrive on this planet. My relationship with them started at a young age when I had my 'invisible' friends playing with me. Growing up, I was interested in playing with others instead of my celestial friends and like many of us I started to forget this relationship until a day in my twenties when I was living in Paris and working for L'Oréal Paris.

Those times were very challenging for me, and I was battling daily stress due to the competitive work environment that I was working in at that time. My ex-husband spent a lot of time working in other countries, so my life was basically 'L'Oréal.' This situation made me feel unhappy when I arrived home every day. I had a nice job, a good husband, friends, money to spend on my trips, but I was feeling so far removed from me, and what my soul's purpose was. I felt a huge distance between what I was living and what I was deep inside of me.

One night, my husband (who was an atheist) was home, and like all night I woke up in the middle of the night to go to the toilet. I was very surprised to find a beautiful big light shining all over the living room. My first reaction was surprise and I thought that I was still dreaming so I came back to the room where my husband was sleeping. The light was behind me whispering in my ears that everything was fine, and I should trust it. This beautiful light introduced itself to me as Gabriel and told me: "You are going to change, you are going to work with us if it pleases you. Your soul is not happy because you are not fulfilling your mission on Earth. Everything is perfect, but you need to move on, and we are going to help you."

I continued thinking it was my imagination. My ex-husband would often say that my mind was brilliant. So brilliant that I could hear voices and give them names. It was not the first time that I had heard voices. Prior to this experience, my research for a peaceful life had led me for a few years to follow Yogananda, and to attend Buddhist & Hinduism teachings in Paris. Additionally, I started an online graduate program in Metaphysics. So, by the time this episode occurred in my life, I had a background in spiritual practices including daily meditation. I still couldn't believe it. I asked them very politely to leave me alone and told them that I was not ready for them.

Gabriel left as I requested, but he told me before leaving: "Remember, love and fear cannot exist at the same time. You need to choose between both. It's up to you."

The next morning, I told my ex-husband about the angel's visit and he suggested that I see a psychiatrist. We had watched the movie "A Beautiful Mind" and in his atheist spirit he was scared that my mind was starting to break. He didn't know that I was attending to all my spiritual practices because for him all these practices were part of a cult, a very dangerous cult.

My relationship with Gabriel was getting stronger and stronger every day until he became my mentor and best friend. One day, he whispered in my right ear (he only speaks into my right ear) and said that I would leave my husband and move to another country. I had a mission on the other side of the Atlantic.

I was scared because my husband was a good man, but our relationship was a relationship of two very good friends for many years. Still, he was my family. One of the reasons I was feeling that way was because of his work. I would only see him on weekends and sometimes every couple of weekends. I started to go deeper into my spiritual path, but he did not agree with it, and was not happy about it.

The messages that I was receiving were coming through more and more often and I couldn't share it with him. We shared very few things in common when that message of divorce arrived.

It took me three years to finally act and leave both my ex-husband and L'Oréal. During this transition, I went to Asia for a couple of months. My father was diagnosed with lupus in my home country Bolivia. The doctors told him that he only had six months to live. At that time, I was utilizing all the knowledge that I was receiving from my spiritual practices. I started to work with clients reading the angel tarot and providing angel therapy, but my husband and in-laws didn't know about it.

2

One night in Singapore, I was sleeping in the common room that I shared with three other girls when the archangel Gabriel said, "wake up, you will receive a message and it's from the Creator." That night has been one of the most wonderful nights I've had in my life.

I saw a flame that started to transform into a pink color and other colors of the rainbow.

I felt warm, my heart was overwhelmed with joy and peace. I felt like I was experiencing nirvana. I felt embraced by this lovely and powerful force. Suddenly, this voice started to talk me telling me that my father was going to be ok, that he was not sick, and I had to trust and believe. I had to tell my father to go to another country for additional medical advice. This magnificent voice told me: "Remember, you are not alone. We are proud of your courage and your actions. From now on, you are going to be surrounded by all the archangels."

I was crying from joy and ecstasy. I've never felt this way before and was overwhelmed by such love and protection. The short story is that I came back to Paris from Asia and brought my dad to Chile for additional medical testing. The creator and the angels were right. He had a treatable liver condition and the test results he previously received were totally wrong. When my father heard what the doctor told him about his health status, he looked at me and said, 'you are a witch.' I do not know who is telling you what to say, but let me tell you something, they are right, and you are lucky to hear them." We were crying from joy and went back to Bolivia where I had another appearance.

This time it related to my path. They (Gabriel and his friends) told me that I needed to be strong. The transition between France and the US would not be easy, and I had to keep my faith and my heart opened to receive their messages.

My divorce was so lovely, friendly, and compassionate, but it was hard to get separated from my family, my friend, my husband. I knew it was part of my lesson and path, so I moved where they told me which was to south Florida. By this time, I was used to following what they were telling me. I knew I could trust them with my life. For some reason, they wanted me to work only with them exclusively, but I didn't know anybody else to share communications with.

Little by little, the doors of teaching Angel Healing opened for me, and I started to teach, and coach people through tarot readings and the messages that I was hearing in my right ear to both individuals and groups.

Another angel miracle I received was my son Gabriel Michael, but that is part of another story. I can just tell you that I got pregnant against the verdict of science. Doctors told me that I couldn't get pregnant. However, I had a natural delivery with no medicine at 38 years old with the angels and my spiritual guides as my doulas.

I believe that if you are reading this book, you can also have this angel gate opened and start to have a magical life with them as I have since I first encountered archangel Gabriel.

In the following chapters, you will learn how to develop this angelic relationship and contact them as part of your celestial team. The angels wish to be part of your life. They are ready to help you solve your challenges, assist you in following your life purpose, achieve your dreams, and to help you meet your Higher Self. Just follow the steps described here, and the angels will take care of everything. Perhaps not in the way that you expect, but surely in divine order. Just believe, trust, and let them do their job.

CHAPTER 1: CONNECTING WITH THE ANGELS

You have probably heard a lot of stories involving the apparition of angels, but how can you work with them? How can you contact them? How can you communicate with them? How can you entertain a relationship with them?

You need to know that everyone can connect with them. We all have the same human and soul equipment to develop and entertain a friendship with our celestial guides.

In this book, I will give you different steps that you can take to have a lasting relationship with them. Please, if something in the book does not resonate with you, I encourage you to continue. If a part of the process below does not resonate with you please skip it, change it, or follow your intuition. What I teach you here, is what has been shared with me from them. The most important thing is what you feel regarding these messages. I know the angels respect 'free will' as your divine right, and I do the same.

Process recommended to establish connection and cultivate a relationship with your angels

1.   Create a sacred space

The first important part of your mission to establish a strong connection with your celestial team is to create a 'sacred space' dedicated to them where you can communicate with your angels. This will be your heavenly place on Earth, and it will be in your home. Angels love to be surrounded by love, harmony, and peaceful energy. In this place, you will honor them and honor yourself feeling relaxed, purified, and with an open your heart you will receive sacred messages.

How can you create a sacred spacet?

a) Clean up your place

Angels feel attracted to places with clean energy where they can unite their spirit with yours. Get rid of junk items that you are holding on to in your home.

Once a year, you can discard the items in your home that you are no longer utilizing. Clutter blocks the angelic energy. Give away what you are not using. This process also will help you to bring abundance to others in need.

b) Bless your home

While you are cleaning up your space, open the windows, let the fresh air come into your home. Play high frequency music, sing a mantra, or pray. The most important thing is that you start to attract high frequencies into your home. You can sing mantras such as Om Shanti, Om Mani Padme Hum, for example. You can also say the names of the archangels: Michael, Gabriel, Raphael, Uriel, Haniel, Zadkiel, Jophiel, Sandalphon, Metatron, Raziel, Azrael, Ariel, Raguel, Jeremiel, Chamuel. You can also say powerful words as love or peace. Let your intuition guide you.

c) Smudge your home

Smudging is and has been an important part of many rituals performed by ancestral cultures. You can bring this ancestral cleansing practice to your space smudging it with Palo Santo or Sage.

You can start smudging at the front door of your place. When you open the door smudge the left side of the room clockwise, and finish smudging at your front door on the right side of your place.

What is important here is that your thoughts attune with the action of cleansing. You can empower this purifying process by visualizing the energy of your home getting cleansed and ridding it of any sad or bad feelings that your home was holding. Remember, everything is energy and every word, action or any feeling created in your sanctuary (your home) remain there. This is an opportunity to release all these energies.

d) Sprinkle blessed water

Additionally, you can also sprinkle holy or sacred water around your place following the same procedure as smudging. From all my trips, I have gathered holy water from sacred places in England, France, Egypt, Jordan, Israel, India, Nepal, Morocco, Greece, Portugal, Spain, Peru, Bolivia, and other powerful places. Only few drops are needed to be sprinkled to change the vibrations immediately.

2.   Create an altar dedicated to your angels

Once you have finished cleaning your home, you can create a special place to connect with your celestial guides: An Angelic Altar. There are no special guidelines for this part of the process, but I will give you some tips in this section:

Cover a small table with a beautiful fabric in your favorite color. Then, you can place a picture or a small statue of your favorite angel(s), spiritual guides, ascended masters, and add crystals, candles, amulets, fresh flowers, a feather, and essential oils. frankincense, myrrh, lavender, rose, sandalwood, jasmine are excellent essential oils for your spiritual practices.

This will be your sacred space where you can attune your energy with the angelic realm. It's very important that you spend a few minutes per day to honor and raise the energy of this space.

3.   Cleanse your energetic bodies

Your mind

Your mind is the home and the seeds of creation are your thoughts. We can talk a lot about peace and happiness but if our thoughts are not aligned with what we are feeling, then communicate with angels or spiritual helpers will be almost impossible. It's important that you understand that we cannot fool the Spirit or ourselves. Being coherent and clear in your actions, thoughts, feelings, and speech are the key to access the higher lessons in your evolutionary path and will empower the communication with your divine team.

What do we need to change about the way we think? First, let's look at the number and nature of our thoughts. We humans have anywhere from 12,000 to 60,000 thoughts per day. But according to some research, as many as 98 percent of those thoughts are the same thoughts that we had the day before. Simply put, we are creatures of habit. Even more significant, researches add that 80 percent of our thoughts are negative.

Negative thoughts are particularly energy draining even if you are not aware of it. Thoughts containing words like 'never,' 'should,' and 'can't,' as well as complaining or whining significantly reduce the production of chemicals that awaken our body. That's why sometimes we feel exhausted.

The good news is that YOU can play a determining role in creating your reality by consciously recognizing a negative or limiting thought. You can 'choose' to change it and replace it with one thought more aligned with your purpose. In this way, you became a co-creator of your own life. The chemicals produced by the body as a reaction to kind thoughts are benefit your entire system, and of course help you to achieve your goals.

What can you do to work on this subject? You can train your mind by practicing meditation, or visualization to soothe the inner chatter and recognize that you are not your thoughts. You are the creator of your existence. You can also sing some powerful mantras or use positive affirmations to change the vibration of your thoughts so that they are aligned with divine communication.

You can walk in nature to reset your mind. Try it and remember, everything starts in your mind.

Your body

Your body houses your soul and is a sacred vessel for your spiritual adventure on planet Earth.

Eating healthy, drinking water, breathing correctly, and working out will ensure that your sacred temple (your body) continues to perform effectively on this human adventure. Remember, only you decide what to eat, drink, how to maintain your body. You are the master of your own universe, and your body is part of it. A little reminder: Your body is the temple of your soul. Take care of it.

Your spirit

I believe that everybody is intuitive. We are all seeds or children of God/Creator/ Supreme Energy. If you intuitively feel that there is negativity around you, use sage or Palo Santo and smudge yourself to cleanse your aura. Your Spirit is always working for your highest good and your own evolution. Try to look every day with your soul eyes and see the blessings beyond the physical plane. We are more than our bodies. Connect with that part of you that never dies. You can use meditation, visualization, past-life regression, and hypnosis to accomplish this goal. Sometimes, we achieve this connection when we get out of our comfort zone and expose ourselves to learn far from our homes, families, and friends. Sometimes, the journey of connection takes place within you. Just trust the divine order of everything in your own life adventure.

4.   Protect yourself

Sometimes, we have people around us that drain our energy. I do not believe these people do it because they are bad beings. Typically, they do not realize that this energy is in them, but you can notice it when you feel drained, sad, tired after hanging out with them. When we do not protect ourselves, these energies can absorb our own energy and feelings of tiredness and sadness can arise in our own being. From this point forward, try to identify those people who drain your energy and start to work with archangel Michael to protect you with his blue light of protection.

There are other situations where you can feel the need of protection as well. At this moment, call archangel Michael and visualize a blue light egg around your aura. It will seal your aura with his celestial energy. A little reminder: trust on archangel Michael. He will do his work. Your job is to keep on faith.

5.   Feeling the presence of angels

The angels are always with us. They are constantly sending us messages. As we live our lives focusing on our human tasks, we forget to feel and see with our soul eyes. Below are a few signs that may indicate the presence of an angel.

- You find white feathers in unexpected places. Sometimes even inside an apartment. This act is a sign from your angels letting you know that your prayers have been heard.
- The temperature in the room has changed suddenly. You can feel warm air surrounding you. You may also experience tingling in your neck.
- You may hear angelic voices trying to give you messages. In my experience, they started communicating in my right ear. This is called, 'clairaudience' and for this we need to practice inner silence.
- You may also experience sensations in your body particularly in your heart. This is the case for the 'clairsentient' when the angels

are near. As a 'clairsentient' you can feel a sensation of love and compassion invading a room and filling your heart.

- You can smell a delicious and mystical fragrance which comes from nowhere. Pay attention to it because normally you smell the same fragrance when they are close to you.
- You may feel the presence of someone in the space that you are in. Sometimes, you can feel a breeze on your back or light hugs.
- You can notice some colors or lights coming from nowhere. They indicate the presence of angels.
- One of their favorite ways to introduce themselves to you is when you are dreaming. At this level, your consciousness is resting while your unconsciousness is liberated from the presence of the ego. The angels know that you will not have any resistance in this state, so they love to show up to you in this state.
- You can see clouds with the shape of an angel in the sky.
- You may talk with someone that has the answer to what you are looking for. The angels can use people as messengers to speak e a message to you.

6.   Invoking the Angels

The angels are here to help us. However, they respect our free will coming only when we call them or in a case of urgency.

They are waiting to connect with you. However, this request must follow these conditions:

a) Your request must respect the free will of others
b) Your request must be positive and not harm others
c) It must not interfere with your or the karma of others. Remember every soul needs to learn some lessons and evolve depending on how the lessons are passed or learned.

Now that you know these conditions, let's look at the different ways you can invoke your angels. Remember to go to the sacred place that you have created when you wish to communicate with them. Here are a few suggestions on how to work with your celestial guides.

• *Pray to your angels*

Praying or talking to your angels is an excellent way of establishing and developing a relationship with them. Each time you contact your angels, your relationship grows. Do you remember how you developed relationships with your friends? I am sure you invested time in calling and talking to them. The same concept applies for your relationship with angels. The more you talk to them, the deeper your relationship develops with them.

You can pray for yourself or others. Be sure that they are always hearing you and working with you. You can pray for people who you do not know or for those who are in distress around the world.

You can also sing, chant, or repeat a mantra using it as a means communication with your angels.

• *Write a letter to your angels*

Sit comfortably in your sacred space. Be sure you are not going to have any distraction during this invocation. Play some angelic music, light a candle, and burn some essential oils or incense.

Start smelling the fragrance of the essential oils or incense as you close your eyes. Inhale and exhale the scent four times to relax and calm the mind. Try to focus on your heart, visualizing a quiet river passing at the level of your heart. Find peace within this image and when you are relaxed begin to focus your attention on the question that you would like to have answered.

Ask the question and take a deep breath as you open your eyes. Now, begin to write the answer that comes to your mind without thinking just writing as you are channeling the answer from the heavenly realm.

If you feel hurt by anyone, send love and compassion to them. Allow yourself to receive their messages with an open heart.

• *Visualize your angels*

You can visualize your angels after a short meditation. Slow down the rhythm of your breath, and begin to visualize shapes, colors, or even the angels hugging you, protecting you with their beautiful light.

• *Call your angels*

Sometimes it's not convenient to call your angels aloud. Especially when you are around other people on the street, in the bank, or any other public place. In this case, just call for them mentally silently asking them "please, angels help me with _____ " or "please, angels protect me."You will be surprised how fast they act.

• *Dream with your angels*

One of the most effective ways to communicate with your angels is through your dream time. When we dream our unconscious is still working without the participation of our ego, so the quality of divine communication is stronger. You can create a dream ritual before going to sleep. Start by giving thanks for all the blessings you have received during the day. Being thankful immediately connects you with the divine beings. Before going to bed, you can say a prayer to work on the astral plane. For example, "angels, please work with me in my dream state tonight, and help me find which direction I should take."

7.   Messages through Angel Cards

One of my favorite ways to ask for messages is through angel cards. You can buy them in most bookstores, online, or you can make your own. The cards will create a wonderful way to receive messages from your celestial team and will help you develop your intuition. Just pick one, three or the cards you need to get the answer you are looking for. Just follow your intuition and let the angels do the rest.

Before you begin angel work, it's important to center yourself by focusing on your breathing and releasing any tension or stress. Breathe in peace and exhale any negative feeling, emotion, or thought that you are experiencing at that moment.

Once you are in a state of peace, place the deck of cards in front of you. Close your eyes and invite your angels to come and guide you on the reading. You can also bring the deck to your heart and charge it with your energy so that you can establish a strong connection with this divine tool. Take a few minutes to attune with your celestial team. Shuffle the card deck thoroughly and as you do, ask the angels for help with a specific question.
Take another deep breath and cut the cards once with your left hand.

Alternate card layouts

I present some layouts that can be helpful at the time to ask to your angels. Explore and feel with one resonate with you:

One Card Spread

The One Card spread is intended to provide a quick answer to a specific situation. Cut the cards with your left hand and simply ask a question. Draw a card and receive the answer. Remember to follow your intuition and feel in your heart what the card's message is trying to answer for you regarding your question. This type of reading is suitable when you are asking about any general situation or you are looking for a yes/no answer. For example: Am I on the right path?

Three Card Spread

Cut the cards with your left hand and place the first three cards in front of you. The card on the left reflects what has happened in the recent past, the middle card relates to the present, and the card on the right side shows the short-term outcome.

This type of reading is suitable when you are asking about an area in your life that is affecting you in this present moment. For example, an overview of your career or love relationship situation.

Five Card Spread

Cut the cards with your left hand and place the first five cards in front of you. This type of reading is useful in decision making. It can give you an advice, or you may discover hidden intentions affecting the situation that you are inquiring about.

It also helps you to see the evolution of a specific situation over time. Take the first card as your present card. The second card will be the situation in 2 months, the third card will reflect the situation in 4 months and goes on until the fifth card.

The Celtic Cross

The Celtic cross is probably the most popular card spread in use today. Traditionally, this is a 10-card spread overlooking important decisions for specific outcomes in the future. I highly recommend this card spread if you have a specific situation in mind that you would like to have more clarification on or requires additional insight. Cut the cards with your left hand and place the first ten cards in front of you.

Weekly Spread

This spread is good for weekly readings. Cut the cards with your left hand and place the first seven cards in front of you with each card representing a day of the week. This is good for receiving daily guidance on things to look out for each day.

Yearly Card Spread

This spread gives an overview of what can happen throughout 12 months. Each card represents a month in the year in the order in which the card was drawn. For example, the first card represents the month of January and so on. Cut the cards with your left hand and place the first of the twelve cards in front of you. Each card tells you what to expect for that month and communicates how you can handle a given situation with the guidance given. This spread is good when you need advice for the entire year. You can also use the 12 cards to focus on a specific topic per month.

CHAPTER 2: ANGELS

The word 'angel' comes from the Greek 'angelos' meaning messenger, and it is the generic name of a collective group of high-energy beings of light whose mission is to maintain the harmony and balance of the Universe. Angels are messengers of the Creator. They contain within them the basic patterns of Creation manifested on Earth's dimension.

Angels are intelligent beings, capable of feeling, they do not have sex. They exist on a vibrational frequency slightly finer than our physical senses. This means that we cannot perceive them with physical senses, but they can perceive us.

Angels are real. Whether modern man chooses to believe it or not, angels exist and have existed before our human generation. If you think about it, there are many things that you cannot see, but just because you cannot see them does not mean they do not exist. For example, electricity. Angels exist in a similar way even though you cannot see them, you can perceive their work when magical things happen in your life.

They work with our souls by aligning them with the universal mind, elevating our spirit, and causing us to remember our truth and unique path. They are here to remind us that we are one with the Great Creator, the Great Spirit, and that we are all children of Infinite Love. When we invoke our angels, we start to work in the company of divine beings who help us with mundane and inspired tasks. In this way, we feel that we are not alone anymore and that everything that happens to us is for a divine reason and is following a divine plan.

The angels act as soul coaches reminding us of our divine purpose. They help us to live according to our truth honoring who we really are. They are always open to connect with you. All you need to do is ask for them and have faith to establish this communion.

Through this collaboration do not feel isolated, and begin to understand that we are not alone. We have never been alone, and that internal magic begins when we accept that their guidance was and is always available to us. We just need to decide to look inside and connect with them from the bottom of our hearts.

Angels want to be our friends and walk with us on our life path. When we open our hearts, our soul eyes, we start to see the little and big miracles in our lives. We begin to play a divine game where we are amazed by the synchronicity of that reality. We understand that our physical reality is created on a higher level of understanding. We become a team player with this celestial team and play an active role with more positivity, motivation, and enthusiasm when sharing our unique gifts with the world. At this moment we experience gratitude. When gratitude is present in our lives, we can uplift our energy to connect immediately with angels.

They help us to connect with the memory of a very ancient origin. We are all children of God. We are children of divinity. This gift illuminates our inner unique talents so that we can share them with the world.

Angels are not limited by form and can travel through multiple dimensions. Therefore, they can appear anywhere at the same time. However, there are instances where they may acquire a denser form when they want to be recognized by humans. They understand that humans in their distracted state only believe what they see with their physical eyes. So, they can appear to them to communicate in some cases.

If your senses were fully developed, you could perceive them as beings of subtle lights penetrating with their energy everything that is around them. You can intensely feel peace that they carry with their presence. We are all walking the path of developing these senses as the Earth is evolving and human as well.

There are many different types of angels. In this journey of your soul's evolution, you will have many encounters. Do not let your doubts and fears block you from the wonderful way of communicating with them. Just surrender to what it is and enjoy the adventure with the celestial beings.

I am sure that while I am writing this I am surrounded by angels and they are helping me to find the right words to convey the information to transmit to anyone that needs it.

How many types of angels are there?

Angels, like humans, belong to families or groups that are differentiated by their vibrational levels. There is no competition in angelic hierarchies. Their spheres are classified by energies and the subtler their energy is, the higher the level within a sphere they are. The best-known manuscripts on angels categorize them in three 'spheres' or 'choirs' since their voices sing to the Creation composing the 'music of the spheres' and is further explained in Hermetic texts as the basic vibration of the Universe. Beginning with those closest to God and ending with those nearest to the physical world, the disposition of angelic choirs is the following:

First sphere:

1. Seraphim
2. Cherubim
3. Thrones

Second sphere:

4. Domains
5. Virtues
6. Powers

Third sphere:

7. Principalities
8. Archangels
9. Angels

Denise Whichello Brown states on her book 'Angel Therapy' the difference between the Spheres:

First Sphere

Seraphim
These celestial beings are said to surround themselves around the throne of God manifesting their glory and singing the music of the spheres. They balance the movements of the planets, stars, and heavens using the power of sound.

Cherubim

They are the custodians of light and stars, guardians of the Arc of the Covenant, and record keepers of the heavens. Although far from our material plane, their light touches our lives and the divine light that they filter from Heaven manifests divine wisdom.

Thrones

They are angels who accompany the planets and manifest union with God. Each planet has its own throne. At this time in our evolutionary development, it is important that we become aware of this throne and the angel of Earth who is the guardian of our planet.

Second Sphere

Domains

They are the beings that manifest the sovereignty of God. They are the regulators of the angelic realm, advising the lower angelic groups that are not as evolved as themselves. Although they receive orders from God and rarely get in touch with individuals, their work is linked to our reality.

Virtues

Manifest the will of God. They are of special importance to us because they can project great levels of divine energy. They are the group of angels manifesting miracles and blessings. The angels who accompanied Jesus during his ascension are believed to be 'Virtues.'

Powers

They are those who manifest the power of God. They are bearers of the conscience of all humanity, those who preserve our collective history. To this category belong the angels of birth and death. They are protectors of the world and believed to be the keepers of the Akashic Records (Records of all the souls' actions on their soul's evolution.)

Third Sphere

Principalities

They are the angels who manifest the dominion of God over nature. They are the devas or guardians of all the great groups from cities and nations to recent human creations, and function like multinational corporations. There are many of these beings dedicated to our planet. They are powerful leaders.

Archangels

Manifest the leadership of God. They belong to a different family of angels, and they will be described extensively in this book. Some command the planetary spirits, others are responsible for the animal kingdom and others fulfill specific tasks in the service of humanity. I see them like the managers of a group of angels with specific characteristics.

Angels

They are the closest to humanity, those who are most concerned with human affairs and in contact with them. Within this category of angels, there are many different ones. The ones that we are most acquainted with are the guardian angels or accompanying angels who are concerned with our spiritual evolution. There are many kinds of angels each serving a different purpose, for example: love, health, career, gratitude, abundance, etc.

CHAPTER 3: ARCHANGELS

Archangels are angels of light leading a group of angels with a similar purpose. They bring understanding and compassion to our lives. They work for the Divine Creator and follow the evolutionary path of all humans. They act in accordance with the universal law of 'free will.' They never force a situation, giving us the right to decide, learn and evolve for ourselves.

As a spiritual practitioner, I have learned that Archangels are pleased to be called anytime you require assistance. In this chapter, I describe 15 archangels you need to work with for different purposes in your life. You will notice that most of the Archangels names end with 'el' – which means 'of God.'

Archangel Sandalphon and his twin brother, Metatron are the only two archangels who once were mortal men and their names do not end with 'el.' Sandalphon lived as the prophet Elijah and Metatron was the wise scribe Enoch.

Before sharing the details of every archangel, I would like to present you with some associations that will allow you to identify the archangels that specifically work with your astrological sign, the elements associated with your sign and the day of your birth. These charts will give you 3 names of the archangels working specifically with you throughout your life.

Archangel for day of the week

Archangel	Day
Michael	Sunday
Jophiel	Monday
Chamuel	Tuesday
Gabriel	Wednesday
Raphael	Thursday
Ariel	Friday
Zadkiel	Saturday

Archangels and Elements

Archangel	Element	Sign	Direction	Color
Uriel	Earth	Taurus, Virgo, Capricorn	North	Green
Raphael	Air	Gemini, Libra, Aquarius	East	White
Michael	Fire	Aries, Leo, Sagittarius	South	Red
Gabriel	Water	Cancer, Scorpio, Pisces	West	Blue

Angel by astrological sign	
Angel	Sign
Ariel	Aries
Chamuel	Taurus
Raphael	Gemini
Gabriel	Cancer
Michael	Leo
Metatron	Virgo
Jophiel	Libra
Azrael	Scorpio
Zadkiel	Sagittarius
Azrael	Capricorn
Uriel	Aquarius
Zadkiel	Pisces

I see the Archangels as the managers of a group of angels. Every archangel has specific responsibilities and tasks regarding humans.

Here there is a description of the 15 archangels including their functions and characteristics. It will help you to identify the archangel or archangels you need to pray for or work with.

Archangels' gender

Throughout history, people have encountered angels in both male and female form. Angels are spirits working specifically with our planet and following earth's physical laws, therefore, they can choose to present themselves with any form or gender.

The Torah, Bible, and Quran (all major religious texts) that often mention angels usually describe angels appearing on earth as males. However, a passage from the Torah and the Bible (Zechariah 5:9-11) describes two genders of angels presenting as two female angels and a male angel to the prophet Zechariah.

Angels have gender-specific energy related to their job or responsibilities on Earth. Doreen Virtue states in her book entitled 'The Angel Therapy Handbook' that "as celestial beings, they don't have genders."

However, angel energies and characteristics allow us to distinguish them with a specific gender. This gender expresses the energy of their vocation. For example, Archangel Michael's protective energy is quite male, while Haniel focusing on the feminine energy of the planet is distinctly female.

In this book, I will refer to archangels as either he or she according to the perception of their gender energy and my own experience of them as well as how they are referred to in existing texts. As your relationship with archangels grows, you will connect with their appropriate energy, and will probably refer to this energy as either he, she, or both.

Archangel Ariel – Lion of God

Archangel Ariel's name means 'lion or lioness of God' and is associated with lions. It also means 'altar.' When Archangel Ariel is around you, you may see sparks, flashes, or twinkles of pale pink light. She is associated with

Nature and is charge with the protection of our planet.

The Angel of Nature

Archangel Ariel is the angel of nature and overseas the protection and healing of plants and animals. Archangel Ariel and the angels of nature guide you to learn about the natural rhythms of the Earth. She attunes you with Earth's seasons and cycles. She supports you in receiving healing from nature in all its forms including healing that comes from rocks, trees, plants, and animals.

Environmentalism

Archangel Ariel is very bound to environmentalism and protects natural environments of all kinds. If you want to work on the field of ecology or anything related to the protection of the environment, then Ariel can guide you.

Totems

Archangel Ariel encourages you to listen to the sounds of nature and to look for messages in the elements of the Earth. She supports you to learn from the signs in rivers, mountains, clouds, seas, lakes, elements of nature, animals (animal allies or totems), stones or crystals (stone or crystal allies or totems), or plants (plant allies or totems). If you want to start working with a totem, call upon Ariel.

Healing animals

Archangel Ariel works along with Archangel Raphael when healing all beings that live on our planet. If you find an injured animal, call upon Archangel Ariel for healing. Archangel Raphael can be called upon alongside Archangel Ariel to reinforce the healing energy.

Embracing courage and releasing blockages

Archangel Ariel is an angel that teaches you how to be courageous so that you can overcome fears and worries. She is a great teacher that encourages you to release any blockage that may prevent you from being the best version of yourself. In doing so, you will walk in your life with more self-confidence and trust the process of life. She is an excellent companion to develop your intuition and psychic awareness.

Embracing life purpose and soul mission

Archangel Ariel also motivates you to reach your full potential by discovering and embracing your true-life purpose and soul mission. Archangel Ariel's teaches you to recognize, follow, and attain your life purpose. She will help you to identify and manifest the actions you need to take to pursue your soul mission. Ariel will infuse consciousness and wisdom into the actions that you take to follow your soul's map. During challenging times, Archangel Ariel reminds you that everything happens for a divine reason and that everything is serving you to fulfill your soul's mission.

Supporting goal setting and problem-solving

Archangel Ariel motivates you to make choices and take actions to develop and create positive changes in your life. Acting as an angel of manifestation, Ariel supports you with goal-setting and problem-solving. Archangel Ariel inspires you to develop new ideas and concepts so you can bring change into your life. These actions will motivate you to make the appropriate decisions that will lead you in the right direction.

Angel of Manifestation and Abundance

Archangel Ariel assists with manifestation of all kinds. In the angelic realm, abundance is your divine right. Archangel Ariel will support you to embrace this right assisting you to achieve your material needs and goals, so that you can vibrate in harmony with the divine abundance that is your divine right.

Each of the archangels has a special place on an etheric level of planet Earth. You can ask them to visit their temples while you are meditating or in your sleep time. Archangel Ariel's spiritual retreat is in Fatima, Portugal. Visit there for healing and light. Archangel Ariel speaks to us through the Root and Heart Chakra.

Archangel Ariel is the patron of activism especially defending the environment, adventurers, animals and pets, campers, ecology, healers, meteorology, park rangers, veterinarians, zoology.

Archangel Ariel usually arrives in your life when you feel you have lost direction and you do not have the tools to continue moving forward. Ariel appears to inspire you and motivate you. She teaches you to use what you already have at your disposition and to embrace change with a more powerful attitude.

Archangel Ariel helps with:

- Prosperity and abundance (love, finances, creativity, health and wealth)
- Discovery, pursuing and fulfilling your life purpose and soul mission
- Environmentalism
- Animal and plant communication
- Manifestation
- Animals especially wild animals
- Revelatory dreams and visions
- Discovery of nature's secrets
- Developing your intuition, psychic abilities and awareness
- Healing especially for animals and plants
- Goal-setting
- Problem-solving
- Overcoming obstacles
- Achieving goals and aspirations

Other names: Auriel, Arael, Ariael
Color: Pale pink
Crystal or gemstone: Aventurine, Crystal Quartz, rose Quartz, Amethyst, Emerald, Jade, Moonstone and pink Tourmaline, Carnelian, Gold, Silver, gold Topaz, peach Aventurine, Opal, Sugilite, Rhodochrosite
Tarot Card(s): Strength
Focus: Connection to nature
Chakra connection: Root and heart
Element: Wind, water, fire, and earth
Direction: North
Trees: All trees
Animals: All animals
Symbols: symbols of the Earth, lion's head, sword and shield, wind
Essential oils: Hyacinth, Hyssop, Jasmine, Neroli, Sandalwood, Frankincense, Myrrh
Day: Tuesday
Astrology/Zodiac: Aries
Flower/Herbs: grapefruit, carrot seed, cedar-wood, ginger, black spruce, black pepper
Ascended masters with similar energy: Coventina, Dana, Glooscap,

Maeve, Sedna
Planet: Uranus

Archangel Azrael – One Whom God Helps

The Hebrew name translates to 'Angel of God', 'Help from God,' or

'One Whom God Helps.' Archangel Azrael helps with big transitions of any kind including loss, separation and death.

Azrael's energy is calm, comforting, supporting and understanding. When Archangel Azrael is around you, you may see sparks, flashes or twinkles of creamy white light.

Transitions and grieving

As humans, change is part of our existence. Archangel Azrael assists you with your personal transitions and transformations. When experiencing change, Archangel Azrael helps you to find wisdom in yourself to create new energies to overcome the chapter you are dealing with.

Transitions can touch your life in many forms, and grief is a reaction to any type of ending. If you are passing through a grieving chapter in your life, call upon Azrael for healing and support. Azrael can support you during the grief process bringing acceptance and love into your heart.

If you are a grief counselor, Archangel Azrael can guide you to find the appropriate comforting words to say to people that you are helping so that they can feel supported in their transition journey.

Mediumship and psychic abilities

Azrael assists people with mediumship and spiritual guidance gifts, helping them to develop their psychic abilities. He also helps them to guide others who come to look for support and need help to develop their psychic gifts.

Finding inner peace

In any transformation point of your life, Archangel Azrael helps you to release any heavy feeling in your heart: unforgiveness, anger, guilt and regret so you can heal your soul and find inner peace to overcome and end the cycle you may be passing through.

Death is a transformation

Archangel Azrael reminds us that death is part of our divine plan and it is a transformation. Azrael's mission is to assist those who are making the transition from physical life to the spiritual realm.

For crossing over, Azrael helps guide them to the light. Azrael brings wisdom and acceptance to our minds and souls. He reminds us that there is a journey after life, and we can embrace this adventure if we trust the process of love that involves death. Azrael helps us to experience a loving and gentle transition releasing from our soul anything that no longer serves us, comforting us so our suffering and fear is removed from our spirit and we can transition in peace. Azrael comforts families and friends whose loved ones have passed.

Connecting with deceased loved ones

Archangel Azrael helps those on the Earth to establish contact with their deceased loved ones. Archangel Azrael and his angels can act as a 'Divine Bridge' to these two different energetic dimensions. Azrael helps to deliver messages of love between both sides of the bridge. Azrael can act as a medium helping you to raise your vibrational rate so that you are able to connect with souls on the other side. Azrael supports mediums to channel information from souls that are making their way back home.

If you are dealing with spirit connection and do not know how to handle this kind of energetic work, call upon Archangel Azrael to help you to understand your gifts and how to support and help the spirits on the other side looking to connect with their loved ones.

Assisting the spirit of the newborns

Archangel Azrael is said to also stand in the background at births, while Archangel Gabriel irradiates love and light energy to the spirit of a newborn during his/her first hours of life outside his/her mother's belly.

Angel of the Akasha

Archangel Azrael is an Angel of the Akasha and works with Archangel Metatron, assisting with the Akashic Records, and they ensure that you are writing your path of life in your own soul book.

Archangel Azrael's spiritual retreat is over the Black Mountains on the borders of England and Wales. Archangel Azrael speaks to you through the Crown chakra.

Archangel Azrael is the patron of the dying and death, caretakers, morticians, grief counselors, pallbearers, funeral home directors.

Archangel Azrael usually arrives in your life to help you with fears related to death and the unknown. Azrael arrives into your life when you are struggling with grief because one of your beloved ones passed to the other side and you are suffering as a result of this separation. Azrael also comes into your life when you need guidance to do your job as a channeler or medium, and to help spirits to transcend.

Archangel Azrael assists you:

- Comforting the dying and grieving
- Crossing over the newly deceased person's soul
- Grief counseling and supporting for the grieving
- Overcoming and understanding transitions and life changes
- Developing mediumship and psychic abilities

Other names: Azrail, Ashriel, Azriel, Azaril, Azrail, Azraille, Azra'eil, Ezra'il, Ezraeli, Izrail, Izrael, Ozryel, Ishmael, Azreil or Ashram
Correct pronunciation: AZ-ray-EL
Color: Creamy White (vainilla color)
Crystal or gemstone: Yellow Calcite, Amethyst, Ametrine, purple Fluorite, Smoky Quartz
Tarot Card(s): Death
Focus: Transitions
Chakra connection: Crown chakra
Element: Ether
Direction: Southwest
Trees: Cedar, Cypress, Pine
Animals: Fox, raven, beetle, crow, dragon, moth and butterfly
Symbols: Half-moon sickle, raven, skull/skeleton
Essential oils: Cypress, Frankincense, Cardamom, Cedar-wood, Sandalwood
Day: Tuesday and Friday
Astrology/Zodiac: Scorpio
Fruits: Blossom of the bean
Flower/Herbs: Acacia, Chrysanthemum, Male Fern, Passion Flower, Sweet Basil
Ascended masters with similar energy: Charon, Enma, Kali, Yama
Egyptian correspondence: Anubis
Greek correspondence: Hecate
Fixed stars: Alphecca
Planet: Saturn, Pluto

Archangel Chamuel – He/She Who Sees God

Chamuel personifies God's love and compassion for all the beings of the planet. He helps you find love and compassion in yourself, so you can mirror others with the same qualities and helps you attract more positive energy around you. Chamuel helps you to boost your vibration and intuition, so you can receive messages or channel information from God or the higher spirits.

His energy is soft, warm, affectionate and loving. When Archangel Chamuel is around you, you may see sparks, flashes or twinkles of pink light.

The angel of Relationships

You can call upon archangel Chamuel when you are looking for new relationships (all kinds of relationships). Chamuel's mission is to help you to find the right people at the right time, so you can fulfill your soul's mission. Relationships are important in our lives. Every person you meet in your life is a piece of the divine puzzle that you are creating. Archangel Chamuel helps you to find these pieces and the lesson these people are bringing to your life. Call upon Chamuel when you want to understand the mission of any person that is in your life. He will help you to go to a higher level of comprehension, understanding, and compassion for your life path and the people that are around you. He helps you build strong foundations for healthy, long-lasting, and meaningful relationships.

Angel of Love

Archangel Chamuel is known as the 'Angel of Love' and he chaperons all the 'Angels of Love.' Archangel Chamuel can help guide you to understand, appreciate, and improve your love relationships with his loving and wise energy. He can advise you on how to find the right people to experience love with while practicing emotional balance. He can also protect you from people who wish to cause you harm by blocking or removing them from your path.

Learn self-love

Feeling in love with others is very pleasant; however, you cannot express true love if you do not love yourself. Archangel Chamuel motivates you to embrace self-love and to dissipate feelings of low self-esteem. Remember true love and true healing start within you.

Finding peace and forgiveness in your heart

One of Archangel Chamuel's missions is to heal a hurting heart.

Chamuel supports you with all of your relationships, especially those that involve life-changing situations: emotional conflicts, separations, and breakups. Call upon him to soothe your spirit and to find peace, forgiveness, and acceptance in your heart. Chamuel can help you when it's difficult for you to forgive or release the past in your heart.

Archangel Chamuel makes your daily life more harmonious. He is the angel that brings peace on Earth and can be called upon to help you to find harmony in your life. Archangel Chamuel can help you get calm and soothe worry, stress, or feelings of panic bringing you back to a state of serenity and inner peace.

Developing creativity

Archangel Chamuel helps you to develop creativity and assists with self-expression. He enables you to express your higher-self through your inspirational work.

Finding lost items and what is aligned for you

Archangel Chamuel plays a similar role as Anthony in Catholicism, who also guides us to find lost items. Archangel Chamuel can see in all directions of time and can help you find your life's purpose; a right relationship for you; a better job; anything, tangible or intangible; everything that you are looking for just with one condition: it must align with your soul's path. He knows God's will for you, so ask for his help. Chamuel serves as an excellent guide to find what is aligned with your soul's map. His messages can be passed by signs and dreams. Be ready to receive instructions.

As 'He who sees God,' Chamuel has almighty vision, and he identifies the connection between everything. Chamuel can also help you to work with your 'third eye chakra' developing it and enhancing the connection with the divine plane and everyone. If you wish to work at a chakra level, you can work with archangel Chamuel connecting your 'third eye chakra,' your 'heart chakra' and your 'sacral chakra' to see the beauty and lessons within the relationships in your life especially with your own life relationship.

Archangel Chamuel and his divine partner, Archeia Charity, serve on the third Ray of Divine Love. Together with the help of the angels of love, they work to spread the flame of unconditional love to all the souls on planet Earth.

Pink is the second color of the heart chakra and teaches us unconditional love. On a physical level, when your heart chakra is in balance, you emanate love and pleasant energy, so your immune system is strong. Developing the heart chakra helps you to express unconditional love for yourself and others.

Archangel Chamuel also works intimately with Paul the Venetian, the Chohan or Master of the third Pink Ray.

Archangel Chamuel's spiritual retreat is over St. Louis, Missouri on the south side of North America. The retreat is called the Temple of the Crystal-Pink Flame.

Archangel Chamuel is the patron of artists, philosophers, peacemakers, metaphysicians, musicians, lightworkers, writers, poets, and all who work from their hearts.

Archangel Chamuel usually arrives in your life when you are dealing with difficulties in your relationships, including love, work and family. Also, when you are struggling with the relationship with yourself and life through the development of self-esteem, self-confidence and self-love.

Archangel Chamuel helps you:

- Strengthening relationship bonds
- Feeling love for the self and other
- Healing a broken heart
- Easing anxiety and bringing inner-peace
- Finding lost objects and items
- Clearing negative emotions and blockages
- Supporting world peace
- Developing your 3rd eye and your vision

Other names: Camiel, Kemuel, Camael, Camiul, Camniel, Johoel, Kemuel, Khamael, Seraphiel, Shemuel
Color: Pink (all shades)
Crystal or gemstone: Rrose Quartz, Flourite, Kunzite, Green Aventurine, Jade, Prehnite
Tarot Card(s): The tower
Focus: Relationships
Chakra connection: sacral chakra (2nd chakra), third eye chakra (6th chakra), and heart chakra (4th chakra)
Ray: 3rd Ray, Pink Ray
Element: Air, developing the higher emotions
Direction: Southeast
Trees: Cherry and Apple
Animals: Deer, dove, rabbit, butterfly
Symbols: A heart that represents love, lotus flower
Essential oils: Rose Otto and Rose
Day: Friday
Astrology/Zodiac: Aries
Ascended master with similar energy: Charity, Serapis Bay, Abundantia, Aine, Artemis, Babaji, Diana, Gaia, Green Man, Kokopelli, Pan, St. Francis, Tara (Green and White), Vila.
Planet: Venus, Mars

Archangel Gabriel – Strength of God

Archangel Gabriel's name means 'God is my strength,' 'strength of God,' or 'the Divine in my strength.' Archangel Gabriel has a special place in my heart because Gabriel is the first angel that has appeared in my life introducing me to the rest of the celestial team. My son's name is Gabriel honoring our friendship in my life and his support on my path to becoming mother.

Archangel Gabriel is known as the 'Angel of the Annunciation,' 'Angel of Resurrection,' 'Chief Ambassador to Humanity,' the 'Angel of Revelation,' and the 'Bringer of Good News, Judgement and Mercy.' Archangel Gabriel is the 'Angel of Harmony, Beauty, Purification and Art,' the 'Angel of Joy' and the 'Spirit of Truth,' and is the awakening Archangel.

Gabriel's energy is delicate, graceful and always brings you hope. When Archangel Gabriel is around you, you may see sparks, flashes or twinkles of baby blue and white light.

Archangel Gabriel represents hope, mercy, revelation, cleansing, freedom, emotions, purity, clarity, communication skills, creativity, inspiration, arts, finding your life purpose, conception, pregnancy, adoption, and emotional healing.

The angel of communication

Gabriel is widely known as the communicator of God in different modalities: writing, art, music, verbal expression, emotional expression, and expression of all kind of communication.

This archangel always communicates with you guiding you in your soul's evolution, sending the messages you need exactly at the right time, so you can grow and make the adjustments needed in your life to follow the directions of your soul's map.

His mission is to pass messages from God to human beings. Call upon him for help with communication of all kinds such as promotional work and networking, arts and media, writing, public speaking, as well as teaching and advocacy work. Call upon Gabriel to promote and support any cause that you are passionate about.

The celestial Public Relationship angel

I see archangel Gabriel as the messenger of messengers, having the role of celestial 'Public Relationships.' When you do not know who to contact for help, ask archangel Gabriel. He will introduce you to the right angel or spiritual guide that can help you with a specific concern.

Gabriel in the Bible

Gabriel is one of two archangels precisely named in the Bible (the other one is Archangel Michael). In the Old Testament's Book of Daniel, Gabriel appears to Daniel to send him and guide him through his visions and dreams. In the Book of Luke, Gabriel appears in the famous scene called the Annunciation. Gabriel announces the births of John the Baptist and Jesus Christ. That's why Gabriel's mission is the divine messenger of God and is why this archangel is the patron saint of communication workers.

The angel of conception, birth, pregnancy, and women's glands

As previously mentioned, Archangel Gabriel is the angel of the 'Annunciation' He guides conceptions, adoptions, pregnancies, births, and the raising of children.

Archangel Gabriel helps women to balance their hormones and helps young women with fertility. If you want to get pregnant, call upon archangel Gabriel to work with you and your heart's desire.

Gabriel surrounds the baby in the womb during pregnancy helping the mother to stay calm, focused, and balanced to create the best ambience for the growth and development of the baby. Archangel Gabriel is present during the birth process irradiating love and hope energy to the newborn. Archangel Azrael is said to stand in the background. For this reason, archangel Gabriel guides all midwives in their role as helpers in bringing life into the world.

Archangel Gabriel guides parents in raising their children so that they can find the appropriate words and actions needed to support their children in following their soul's mission.

The archangel of children

If you feel the call to work with children, please ask Gabriel to help and guide you towards this beautiful work.

As the Archangel of children, Gabriel can guide you to nourish your inner child. Your inner child represents the original version of yourself. This beautiful being is still within you and carries the capacity to reproduce experiences of joy and higher feelings of innocence, wonder, and playfulness. If you want to work with issues relating to traumas stemming from your childhood, Gabriel is an excellent counselor.

Following your personal truth

Archangel Gabriel motivates you to find and follow your personal truth and motivates you to live that truth courageously. Living your truth will help you to find and express your unique gifts, talents and abilities. When you fulfill your life purpose, you make a worthwhile contribution to humanity.

Archangel Gabriel helps you to express your truth and to listen to your inner voice heightening your intuition.

Celestial connection and guidance

Archangel Gabriel coaches you when you are meditating, invoking angelic help, during your rituals, ceremonies and meditations. He guides you through your dreams to open yourself to the messages you are receiving on an astral level. Gabriel helps you to interpret your visions and dreams.

The angel of creativity

Gabriel is the angel of creativity. Gabriel's energy encourages joyfulness, spiritual upliftment, and peace, so you can feel divinely inspired to create any sort of conception coming from your higher self. When you feel the call to create, call upon archangel Gabriel beginning with a short meditation and attuning with his energy before conceiving any project.

Archangel Gabriel is the Archangel of the West ruling over the element of Water, and relates to the astrological signs of Cancer, Scorpio and Pisces. Archangel Gabriel also is the angel of the fourth ray of Harmony radiating white Light.

Water is connected to your emotions and Gabriel helps to purify negative emotions, unhealthy patterns and beliefs clearing your mind and emotions. You can call upon him to clear and purify your body from toxins and clear your mind of negative or impure thoughts, beliefs, and mind-sets.

One way to connect and work with Archangel Gabriel is through positive affirmations as they motivate you to uplift your spirit and change your mindset. Another option is to sing mantras or medicine songs, meditate, or use visualizations.

Archangel Gabriel and Hope are archangel and archeia of the fourth Ray of Purity and the Ascension Flame. Together with the seraphim, their angels guard the immaculate concept of the God design for everyone and reinforce the flame of hope around the world. White is color of this Ray and Serapis Bay the Chohan overseeing the purity of this ray.

The etheric retreat of Archangel Gabriel and Hope is located in the etheric plane between Sacramento and Mount Shasta, California, USA. Visit this spiritual retreat to receive clarity about questions you may have regarding your life. Also, to receive purification of the mind, body and spirit. In addition, you can visit the retreat to release you of any old patterns and faulty beliefs that are not serving you anymore. He helps to connect you with your children and your own inner child and brings hope into your life.

Archangel Gabriel works with the Throat Chakra (5th chakra) and the thyroid gland. Work with him to improve any communication concerns that you may have and for connection with the celestial realm.

Archangel Gabriel is the patron of those whose life calling involve art and communication, artists, designers, architects, journalists, writers, communicators, musicians, authors, reporters, coaches, healers, psychics/clairvoyants, teachers, facilitators, lecturers, actors, singers, songwriters, dancers, spiritual leaders, motivational speakers, orators, philosophers, physicists, and poets.

Archangel Gabriel usually arrives in your life when you begin to question your mission as soul and human being, and you start to awaken to new possibilities of existence. Gabriel also enters your life when you are connecting with your spiritual team to embrace your soul's plan.

Archangel Gabriel helps you:

- Expressing your truth
- Honoring your individuality
- Listening to your intuition and inner-voice
- Overcoming procrastination
- Guiding your spiritual life
- Supporting your connection with the spiritual realm
- Discovering and embracing your life purpose
- Bringing hope, joy, happiness and fulfillment
- Inspiring creation of projects
- Getting pregnant and child birth
- Raising children
- Releasing old patterns and beliefs, negative habits, past hurts and old memories
- Receiving messages through dreams and interpreting them
- Working with your inner child

Also known as: Lord Gabriel
Color: Baby blue and white
Crystal or gemstone: Aquamarine, Clear Quartz, Fluorite, Geodes, Moonstone or Pearls, Celestite, Angelite, Blue Calcite, Tanzanite,

Turquoise
Tarot card: The empress, The hanged man
Focus: Connection, messages, creativity, hope
Chakra: Throat chakra (5th chakra) and sacral chakra (2nd chakra)
Ray: 4th Ray
Element: water
Direction: West
Trees: Almond, Bay, Coconut Palm, Hazel, Papaya and Weeping Willow
Animals: Crabs, shellfish, dog, seagull, dove, owl and white peacock
Symbols: Dove, nine-pointed star, banner, scroll, sword, trumpet
Essential oils: Camphor, Jasmine, Frankincense, Sandalwood
Day: Monday
Astrology/Zodiac: Cancer
Flowers/Herbs: White Lilies
Ascended masters with similar energy: Paul the Venetian, Confucius, Jesus, Mother Mary Queen of Angels, Siddhartha, Gautama Buddha
Egyptian correspondence: Hathor
Greek correspondence: Diana
Fixed star: Sirius, Castor and Pollux and Procyon
Planet: Moon

Archangel Haniel – Grace of God

Archangel Haniel's name means 'glory of God' or 'grace of God.' Haniel is known to be the 'Angel of Intellectual Activity.' Doreen Virtue, in her book 'Archangels and Ascended Masters' states, that in ancient Babylon, a group of men known as 'priests-astronomers' worked with metaphysics and psychic activities including astrology, astronomy, moon cycles, and other rituals for their spiritual work. One of the archangels evoked on those rituals was archangel Haniel, associated with the planet Venus.

Kabbalistic texts mention Archangel Haniel as the archangel who accompanied Enoch to the spirit world where he evolved to Archangel Metatron. When Archangel Haniel is around you, you may see sparks, flashes or twinkles of bluish white light.

Angel of intuition and psychic abilities

Archangel Haniel is the 'Angel of Intuition' and her energy vibrates with the knowledge of ancestral healing, ancestral medicine, ancestral wisdom, psychic abilities and intuition.

Haniel empowers spiritual practitioners to work and enhance their intuition and self-awareness in divination guiding them to develop their psychic abilities, spiritual talents, clairvoyance and healing gifts. Her energy is graceful, calming, reassuring, and gentle. Haniel speaks with such soft and comforting voice to guide you to help you to develop and bloom your intuition and psychic abilities.

Bringing beauty, harmony, and peace in your life

Call upon Archangel Haniel to bring beauty, harmony, balance, pleasure, harmonious relationships, peace, serenity, and inspiration into your life. Haniel helps you to see beauty and perfection around you, even in difficult moments. Her energy motivates you to release and heal negative emotions such as envy, guilt, anger, jealousy, resentment and judgement.

Teaching you your strengths and self-love

Archangel Haniel encourages you to become empowered, embracing your strengths, so you can use them wisely while respecting and honoring yourself and others. Haniel helps you to gain self-confidence. She acts as a life coach that motivates you to enjoy life, bringing harmony, peace, and balance in your life. Haniel will support and teach you to take care of yourself, respecting and loving your body and spirit. Haniel reminds you that you are a powerful and divine being with so many unique gifts.

The angel of the moon

Archangel Haniel vibrates with the energy of the Moon. She helps you to boost your inner gifts. Haniel empowers you to shine within you to embrace your own shadows and learn from them, so you can bring healing into your life and the lives of others. Archangel Haniel teaches you to respect the cycles of the Moon and honor your own natural cycles and rhythms.

Regulating women's cycles

Archangel Haniel helps women with regulating monthly cycles and during ovulation. Call upon Haniel when you are suffering from painful menstruation and hormonal imbalances of all kinds. She offers help to women, restoring balance within their bodies during and after pregnancy, as well as during menopause.

The angel of Divine Feminine teaching us polarity

Haniel teaches lessons of duality and polarity. She also oversees mythology and religions of all kinds. As the angel of Divine Feminine, Haniel can particularly help with women's issues. Likewise, she can also guide men as them also have feminine energy.

The wisdom of our ancestors

Archangel Haniel reminds you of the wisdom of your ancestors and helps to bring back their insight and apply it into any kind of healing practices and/or remedies. Call upon Haniel to connect with your ancestors and remember the medicine that your lineage has been carrying. It will be a gift for you, your children and others.

Archangel Haniel is the patron of astrology, astronomy, charity workers, clergy, diplomats, healers, intuitive people, light workers, relief workers.

Archangel Haniel's spiritual retreat is above the mountain ranges of Puno in Peru. Visit the retreat when you want to bring beauty, hope and balance in your life. At a chakra level, Haniel works on the Sacral Chakra (second chakra) and the Heart Chakra (fourth chakra).

Haniel usually arrives in your life when you need clarity in your life and need to see the situations with a different perspective.

Archangel Haniel assists with:

- Soul expression
- Spirituality and developing spiritual gifts and abilities
- Strengthening your intuition and trust
- Grace, balance and harmony
- Emotional intelligence
- Dignity and integrity
- Moon connection and healing
- Disperse and healing negativity
- Staying calm, poised and centered
- Inner-strength, self-belief and self-confidence

Also known as: Anael, Aniel, Anafiel, Hamiel, Hamael, Hanael, Onoel, Omoel, Daniel
Color: Bluish white

Crystal or gemstone: Moonstone, Angelite, Howlite, Selenite, Crystal Quartz
Tarot Card(s): The High Priestess and The Moon
Focus : Find passion, grace, beauty and harmony in your life
Chakra : Sacral (second chakra) and heart (fourth chakra)
Element: Water
Trees: Bleeding Heart, Cinquefoil, Cotton, Holly, Olive, Peace Lily, Palm, Rose, Sage
Animal : Wolf, deer, sparrow
Symbols: Full moon, heart of compassion, rainbow, sunbeams
Essential oils: Basil, Marjoram, Coriander, Jasmine, Cardamom, Neroli and Sandalwood
Day: Monday and Friday
Astrology/Zodiac: Taurus, Libra
Flowers/Herbs: Rose (symbolizing spiritual growth, enlightenment, love and beauty)
Ascended masters with the same energy: Master Hilarion, Sanat Kumara, Lady Radiant, St. John of God, Spider mother
Planet: Moon and Venus

Archangel Jeremiel – Mercy of God

Jeremiel means 'mercy of God' or 'God's mercy' or 'Lord of Souls awaiting resurrection,' and is known as the 'Angel of Transition and Change,' 'Angel of Life Review,' and the 'Angel of Visions and Dreams.' Archangel Jeremiel enlighten your life so you can have a new perspective and make good decisions to bring positive changes in your life. When Archangel Jeremiel is around you, you may see sparks, flashes or twinkles of purple light.

Understanding challenging situations

Jeremiel's energy is supporting, lovingly teaching us compassion and mercy. You can call upon him to help you to understand challenging situations in your life, so you can resolve them wisely respecting the others and the divine order.

Angel of Hope

Jeremiel is referred as the Angel of Hope. He is one of the Archangels who accompany those who are crossing over to the spiritual realm. Jeremiel helps you to understand that there is hope after a material transition, and there is not separation after death.

Life review's angel

Archangel Jeremiel reviews our lives with us after we have crossed over and helps us to re-adapt and adjust to our spirit bodies. Jeremiel also helps people review their life on Earth. He helps to make changes and adjustments to fulfill your soul's mission, so you don't need to wait until your physical passage to have a life review.

He helps you to see the lessons on every challenging situation in our life, for example: changing your job after many years, getting divorce, getting separated from somebody you love, leaving your parents' home, etc. Archangel Jeremiel reminds us that we always have choice. He helps you to understand that you are always creating your life with the decisions you make. Archangel Jeremiel motivates you to make positive life choices and life adjustments, so you can maximize your opportunities creating positive outcomes in the future. He stimulates you to follow the right path while fulfilling your life purpose.

See situations with another perspective

Archangel Jeremiel empowers you to see with clarity the situations and circumstances of your life from a different and elevated perspective. Jeremiel can help you to show you the teachings and blessings within each experience of your life.

Trusting the present moment

Archangel Jeremiel is an excellent advisor when you are concerned about the future in any way. Jeremiel will help you to trust in the present moment and to release fears, worries and anxieties regarding the future. He will remind you that when you trust, you cannot experience fear. Jeremiel will support you to trust on the divine process and to believe in life. Call upon Jeremiel to help you to contemplate yourself and your future from a greater outlook.

The Keeper of Karmic Contracts

Archangel Jeremiel teaches us to take responsibility for ourselves, our thoughts and actions, knowing that there is always a divine order and divine justice. As we take responsibility of our actions, we clean and cure karma issues. Jeremiel, being the 'Keeper of Karmic Contracts' helps archangel Metatron in guiding us to find the way to break, conclude and release these contracts in divine order respecting the free will of all souls.

Prophetic dreams and visions

Archangel Jeremiel supports us to experience prophetic dreams and visions, guiding us on an astral level to see what we cannot see on a daily basis and understand those messages to apply it in our life. Because of this quality, he can help you to develop and improve your clairvoyance skills and psychic abilities. For these characteristics, Archangel Jeremiel helps you to work and balance your Third Eye Chakra.

Archangel Jeremiel's spiritual retreat is above the Valley of the Death in Egypt. Visit the retreat when you want to review your life and find the courage to make changes in your life. At a chakra level, Jeremiel works on the Third Eye Chakra (sixth chakra).

Archangel Jeremiel is the angel of socials workers, legal advisors, counselors, life coaches, psychologists and therapists.

Archangel Jeremiel usually arrives in your life when you want to make a life review and you are passing through a challenging situation and need to see with clarity to make decisions to follow your path.

Archangel Jeremiel helps you:

- Enhancing clairvoyance gifts and intuition
- Bringing hope and light in our lives
- Trusting the future and enjoy the present moment
- Developing spiritual awareness and interpreting prophetic dreams and visions
- Reviewing your life and making life choice
- Overcoming life changes and transitions of all kind
- Being responsible for our actions
- Releasing the past

Also known as: Jeremeel, Jerahmeel, Hieremihel, Ramiel, Remiel.
Color: Purple
Crystal or gemstone: Fluorite, Amethyst, Rhadochrosite, Garnet
Tarot card: The judgement
Focus: Life review, dream interpretation and karma issues
Chakra: Third eye (sixth chakra)
Element: Water and ether
Trees: Chamomile, Passion Flower, Valerian, Kava Kava
Animals: Bee, scorpion
Symbols: Scorpio, open book, scribe
Essential oils: Valerian, Chamomile, Mhyrr, Lavender
Day: Tuesday
Astrological /Zodiac: Pisces
Ascended master with similar energy: Toth, Anubis, Nada, Pallas Athena, Portia, Kuan Yin, Elohim Cyclopea
Planet: Jupiter and Uranus

Archangel Jophiel – Beauty of God

Jophiel's name means 'Beauty of God.' Her energy is soft, cordial, pleasant, and elegant. Jophiel always reminds us that is positive to change our inner talk and transform it in a positive way. Archangel Jophiel motivates us to maintain positive thoughts.

Her mission is to bring beauty to all aspects of life, including thoughts, feelings, personal self, home and office. When Archangel Jophiel is around you, you may see sparks, flashes or twinkles of yellow light.

Understanding the connection of your life

Archangel Jophiel helps you to understand the connections of all the circumstances and situations of your life, so you can see the big picture and realize that everything is perfect and in divine order. There is beauty in all paths. You just need to open the eyes of your soul and accept that beauty is your divine right.

Teaching beauty, self-confidence and love your body

Jophiel will support you as life coach teaching you self-confidence so you can feel sure about yourself and others. This confidence will grow as your inner beauty grows. Jophiel will show you that beauty resides inside of you and you can express beauty from your heart. Jophiel can also boost you to appreciate beauty around you, everywhere in our environment.

Archangel Jophiel helps to heal negative body images. She encourages you to be in peace with your body taking care of it as the temple of your soul. Jophiel can help you if you are struggling with anorexia, bulimia or any eating disorder issues.

Angel of Wisdom and Illumination

Archangel Jophiel is the 'Angel of Wisdom and Illumination.' Jophiel helps you to expand your understanding regarding your experiences in life and the purposes of them. This understanding brings a confident and hopeful approach to life.

Archangel of wisdom and concentration

As the Archangel of the Second Ray, of Love and Wisdom, Jophiel brings us the gifts of intuition, wisdom, bliss, pleasure, attention, awareness, revitalization, regeneration, and soul illumination. Jophiel will guide you to use emotional intelligence in your relationships with others and yourself. She will encourage speaking in an enlightened manner. Call upon Archangel Jophiel when you need assistance in all aspects of education, learning, analyzing, concentration, mental agility, research, data retention, tests and examinations, and help with absorbing new skills and talents.

Assisting with inspiration and creativity

Jophiel assists you with inspiration and creativity lighting up your mind and spirit, so you can bring original outcomes. Archangel Jophiel is the Archangel of beauty and art, is also known as the 'Patron of Artists.' She assists with artistic projects illuminating and inspiring us in your artistic ventures.

Feng Shui Angel

Archangel Jophiel is known also as the 'Feng Shui Angel.' Call upon Jophiel to guide you on how to organise your home so energy flows affecting positively your energy levels, mood, sleep patterns, and even health.

The diplomatic angel

Archangel Jophiel is a diplomatic angel. She assists leaders, politicians, ambassadors and people of power and influence, to speak with dignity honoring values of peace and harmony. Call upon her when you want to find a harmonious speech respecting everyone's perspective.

Archangel Jophiel and Christine are the archangel and archeia of the second Ray of Wisdom and Illumination. These twin flames amplify the Christ consciousness within angels, elementals and men. The Chohan Lanto oversees the yellow Ray of Wisdom and Illumination.

Archangel Jophiel's spiritual retreat is on South of the Great Wall of China. You can come in your meditation or dream time to receive illumination, wisdom, and/or to be helped with your studies/teachings. Archangel Jophiel oversees the expanding of the Solar Plexus Chakra (third chakra) helping us to shine and to show the beauty that is inside of us. This chakra illuminates your mind and fills you with energy.

Archangel Jophiel is the patron angel of architects, artists, art historians, art museum curators and benefactors, art teachers, community beautification groups, fashion designers and models, film directors and production crews, gardeners, interior decorators, beauticians and hair stylists, Feng Shui practitioners, masons, painters, philanthropists, photographers, sculptors, visionaries, wedding planners, leaders, politicians, ambassadors and people of power and influence.

Archangel Jophiel usually arrives to your life when you need to see beauty in challenges or difficulties; to overcome challenges learning the lesson and continue your path with a positive mind set. Also, when you need to increase your ability to learn and to assimilate information. And when you need to develop self-esteem and self-confidence.

Archangel Jophiel helps you:

Raising self-esteem and self-confidence
- Having another perspective of a difficult situation
- Appreciating beauty around you and inside of you
- Being more diplomatic in your speech
- Aligning you to your Higher-self
- Supporting soul awakening and soul illumination
- Inspiring you and helping you to create
- Developing positive thoughts
- Strengthening mental agility, concentration and gaining of wisdom
- Absorbing new skills and talents
- Supporting all aspects of education, study and learning, concentration, information retention, examinations and tests
- Healing negative body images and beliefs
- Expressing your own unique beauty

Also known as: Iofiel, Iophiel, Jofiel, Zophiel
Colour: Yellow
Crystals: Golden Labradorite, Citrine, Rose Quartz, Moonstone, natural sea Shell
Tarot card: The devil, The star
Focus: Beauty of life, patience, wisdom and illumination
Chakra: Solar plexus (third chakra)
Ray: Second Ray, of Love and Wisdom
Element: Fire
Trees: Alfalfa, Allspice, Amaranth, Apple, Apricot, Avocado, Cabbage, Cardamon, Cherry, Cinnamon, Corn, Daisy, Geranium, Gourd, Grape, Henna, Hibiscus, Jasmine, Licorice, Lilac, Lime, Lemon, Oat, Orange, Orchid, Papaya, Peach, Pear, Primrose, Rose, Sassafras, Strawberry, Sunflower, Tomato, Vanilla, Wheat
Animals: bee, bison, cougar/panther, cow, fox, frog, hummingbird, parrot, peacock, seals and sea lion, swan, tiger
Symbols: quarterstaff, swan, sunflower
Day: Friday

Astrological / Zodiac: Libra
Ascended master with similar energy: Kuthumi, Archeia, Aphrodite,
Athena, Giver, Lakshmi, Mary Magdalene, Oshun, Vesta
Flowers/Herbs: All yellow flowers
Planet: Venus and Saturn☐

Archangel Metatron – The One Who Guards

Metatron means 'The One who guards' or 'The One who serves behind
God's throne.' He is one of the two brothers who were once human but
ascended into Angels. Because of this, his energy is more human than any
other angel. Metatron is one of two archangels whose names don't end in
the -el suffix, which means 'of God.' That's because Metatron and
Sandalphon were both human prophets: Enoch and Elijah, who were
rewarded with ascension into the archangel realm. When Archangel
Metatron is around you, you may see sparks, flashes or twinkles of white

and pink with green swirls light.

The angel who understands human worries

Metatron understands human worries and difficulties being more direct and analytic in giving human advice. You can call on him when you need help to reach your goals and work on manifesting on Earth plane what is in your mind and heart.

Metatron acts as a bridge between humans and the Divine.

The Angel of Life and the Akashic Records

Archangel Metatron is called the 'Angel of Life,' he is the guardian and overseer of the 'Tree of Life' and the one that takes notes of all accomplishments of your soul. He passes this information on the 'Book of Life,' 'Library of Light,' 'Collection Unconscious,' 'Universal Mind,' 'Soul's Record' known as the 'Akashic Records.' He is the 'Scribe of God,' recording everything that happens on our planet, with a complete memory of every being on Earth and every person's actions. Archangel Metatron can also help you with your writing skills.

The chief angel of Kabbalistic traditions

Archangel Metatron is the chief angel of Kabbalistic traditions guiding the paths of humans. Archangel Metatron transmits wisdom and understanding to all of those who are ready.

The angel helper of children

Archangel Metatron is the angel helper of children aiding them and their parents on children's developmental problems, wisdom, adaptability to new cycles of childhood, and guiding them to embrace their unique gifts. Archangel Metatron also works with the Indigo, Crystal, and Rainbow children; those who have incarnated to awaken our planet. He also guides children and adult sensitives to their human mission always protecting them from heavy energies generated on this planet.

Helping you to socialize

Sometimes, our children or ourselves have difficulties to socialize because we do not know how to express and live our unique gifts. Metatron can help if you or your child need assistance with socialization.

The angel of Sacred Geometry

Metatron is the angel of Sacred Geometry and is involved in anything related to energy work, quantum physics and mathematics. He works with the Merkabah cube for any kind of healing even for clearing and codification. Metatron also helps to cut cords and attachments starting with our thoughts. These attachments can be related to relationships, objects, situations, habits, etc. It's said that Metatron has helped to build the ancient sacred temples in our planets, including the pyramids, Machu Pichu, Stonehenge and other places of high frequency on Earth.

The teacher of esoteric knowledge

For all of his qualities, Metatron is a teacher of esoteric knowledge. If you want to receive knowledge from a celestial master, call upon archangel Metatron. He will teach you to use your spiritual abilities for the highest good for yourself and others, so you can make a positive difference to the world in your own unique way. Metatron encourages you to be who you truly came here to be.

Calming down stress

Metatron helps you to calm down at stressful moments, so you can find peace to make the correct decisions. He helps you to stay focus, disciplined, and organized with your projects, taking the right actions to achieve your goals.

Archangel Metatron oversees the Stellar Gateway Chakra of people and the planet. Metatron opens the portal of the Soul Star Chakra activating and initiating the 'enlightenment' of our bodies in all levels. Metatron is an excellent helper to connect ourselves to the Source as he is the leader of the ascension of our planet.

Archangel Metatron's spiritual retreat is on Findhorn in Scotland. Visit the retreat to understand deep and profound esoteric lessons as sacred geometry.

Archangel Metatron is the patron angel of accountants, archivists, babysitters, bankers, children, child psychologists, librarians, nannies, pediatricians, sacred geometry, scribes, storytellers, teachers.

Archangel Metatron usually arrives to your life when you are feeling the call to spiritual and esoteric teachings, finding balance with your spirit, mind and body. He arrives also when you need to clear away lower energies that are not allowing you to live fully your life purpose and soul mission.

Archangel Metatron helps you:

- Manifesting and achieving your goals
- Connecting with Source
- Helping with spiritual awakenings
- Developing your spiritual gifts
- Finding and maintaining balance in your life
- Clearing away lower energies
- Cutting cords and attachments to people, material items, and destructive behaviors
- Working with children and special spiritual gifted kids and adults
- Understanding sacred geometry and spiritual symbols
- Socializing with others

Also known as: Metratton, Mittron, Metaraon or Merraton
Color: White and pink with green swirls
Crystal or gemstone: Watermelon Tourmaline, Agate, Crystal Quartz, Topaz, Moonstone, Kyanite, Labradorite
Tarot card: The fool, The chariot
Chakra: Soul star chakra, stellar gateway chakra
Focus: Spiritual evolution, working with children, enlightenment, light body activation and ascension
Trees: Celery, Chamomile, Coconut, Gotu Kola, Hemp, Lavender, Passion Flower, Poppy, Valerian, Walnut
Symbols: Books, Clouds, rainbows
Essential oils: Coconut, lavender, passion flower
Day: Monday
Astrological / Zodiac: Virgo
Animals: Ant, crane, elephant, goldfish, goose, kitten, mouse, ostrich, stork
Ascended master with the same energy: Devi, Ganesh, Ho Tai, St. Nicholas
Planet: Earth

Archangel Michael – He Who is Like God

Archangel Michael's name means 'who is Like God.' Archangel Michael is probably the most know of all the angels and archangels. He has been sainted. Many churches have his name, and he appears in texts of the Bible and other sacred texts. There are many sculptures and portraits of Michael in many places around the planet. Michael has two main tools: a sword and a shield. This is because Michael's primary purpose of eliminating the ego and fear of our souls and lives; and protection of any circumstances.

Archangel Michael is the Archangel of the South ruling over the element of Fire and relates to the astrological signs of Aries, Leo and Sagittarius. Archangel Michael represents the energies of truth and protection. When Archangel Michael is around you, you may see sparks, flashes or twinkles of royal blue light.

Protection

Archangel Michael is the 'protector angel' and is known as the 'Protector of Humanity,' 'Prince of the Archangels,' and the 'Defender of the Faith.' Michael shields us immediately when we need it so we can feel sure and accompanied in challenged situations. You can call on him for protection when you're feeling scared, sense any dark energies, and would like him to clear your personal space or property.

Michael can help in any kind of protection you may need:

- Protecting your body, your material belongings, your loved ones, and your reputation
- Protecting you while you are in your vehicle from having potential accidents
- Spiritual protection from psychic attack and all negative emotion coming from others or yourself
- Protecting homes from robbery or lower energies

Strength and courage

Archangel Michael is the protector of all humanity, and he is the archangel you can call upon when you are looking to empower yourself and gain confidence to make the right decisions in your life. If you want to find your life purpose, respect and be respected, change the direction of your life, strength in your commitments, motivation, positive self-talk, energy, courage, vitality, the ability to take full control and responsibility for your life, call upon Michael. He will be on your side shining his powerful energy, so you can overcome any challenging situation in your life.

Clear out low energies and cuttings cords

Archangel Michael and his 'angels of light' work for us in removing energy that doesn't belong to us and keep us tied to others' energy.

Sometimes we hold to toxic relationships and toxic behaviors keeping unhealthy relationships, suffering coming from the past, psychic attack, negative mind-sets and beliefs, drama, trauma and abuse. All these stay in your spirit as a weight blocking you to advance and move freely on your life adventure. Emotional baggage doesn't allow us to be free and enjoy our gifts and the gifts of others. In consequence, your energy slows down causing you emotional stress, and blockages enter within your energy system. Archangel Michael brings angelic empowerment helping you to release your fears, traumas, soul's pain so you can reach your true potential and fulfill your life purpose. Michael also helps us to cut cords that keep us living in the past.

Break down barriers and respecting diversity

Archangel Michael is supporting the unity of all nations in the world, breaking down barriers that separate countries, families and individuals. Call upon him for the respect of the diversity and the communion of all the members of families and countries.

Fixing machines and tech items

Archangel Michael helps to fix machinery, engines, vehicles and any form of technological items, such as: computers, faxes, telephones, washing machines, and other mechanical items.

Speaking our truth

Archangel Michael helps us to respect our truth respecting our integrity. He motivates us to find the courage to be faithful to our truth honoring ourselves. Michael also helps you to overcome the fear of speaking in front of others, especially when you need to present yourself to an auditorium or group of people. Call upon him to be aligned with your inner truth and embrace who you are in front of others. Archangel Michael encourages leadership qualities.

The lawyer of the heaven

Michael is the angel working for Divine Justice and helps anyone with legal concerns. Call upon him when you need legal assistance at any moment and when you are required to sign a formal document. Michael is also the angel of the police officers and any job of justice and order.

Career and passions

Archangel Michael guides those who feel stuck in their career path and/or life purpose and realigns you with your passions and inner gifts. If you want to change your career, if you are looking for a job, if you are looking for change of position at your job, if you are going to a job interview, call upon archangel Michael. He will boost you to make important changes on your career life.

Archangel Michael is the Prince of the Archangel. He is in first line of the guardian angels of protection. His divine complement is Archeia Faith. Both are archangels of the first Ray Power, Protection, and Faith. El Morya is Chohan of the Blue Ray of Protection.

Archangel Michael's esoteric retreat is called the 'Temple of Faith and Protection,' in the etheric realm over the Canadian Rockies, near Banff and Lake Louise, Alberta, Canada, and extending over the border of the United States. Visit this retreat during your dreams or meditation to look for protection, to find self-esteem and courage, alignment with your truth, inner gifts and life purpose.

Michael is the archangel that oversees the Third Eye Chakra (sixth chakra), focusing on your mind and can be called upon to help with mental challenges, to help construct alternative choices for any outcomes in your life, and to help with decision making.

Archangel Michael is the patron angel of auto racing, basketball, body builders, dancers, firemen, football, health and fitness, military, police, protectors of truth and justice, lawyers, human resource staff, sports, and competition, sun and beach worshippers, surfer dudes and dudes, wrestlers.

Archangel Michael usually arrives in your life when you need protection and energy on your path. Also, when the environment in which you live (including relationships) needs to be cleared away. Michael is present as well when you need to work on your job/career.

Archangel Michael helps with:

- Courage
- Energy and vitality
- Legal aspect
- Life purpose

- Self-esteem and inner truth
- Public speaking
- Protection of any kind
- Motivation
- Direction and leadership
- Space clearing
- Spirit release
- Machines and tech items repair

Also known as: Beshter, Mikall, Mika'il, Sabbathiel, Saint Michael, Sabbathiel Saint Michael, Lord Michael.
Color: Royal Blue and royal purple
Crystal or gemstone: Lapis Lazuli, Sugalite, Sodalite, Angelite, Rainbow, Hematite and all blue crystals and gemstones
Tarot card: The emperor, The wheel of the fortune, The world
Focus: Protection, faith, will of God, power, energy
Chakra: Third eye chakra (sixth chakra)
Ray: First Ray, of Power, Protection, and Faith
Element: Fire
Direction: South
Trees: Laurel, Acacia, Angelica, Ash, Banana, Bay, Black Cohosh, Black Pepper, Carrot, Cashew, Chili Pepper, Cinnamon, Date, Fennel, Fig, Gingseng, Nutmeg, Olive, Onion, Patchouli, Rose, Ruda, Saffron, Sesame, Sunflower
Animals: Bear, dull cardinal, cock, eagle, condor, falcon, hawk, lion, black panther, black cat, jaguar
Symbols: Sword and shield, eagle, condor, flag, lion, black panther, medieval armor, scales of justice
Essential oils: Frankincense, Myrrh, Ruda, Anise Star, Aniseed, Pepper, Cajeput, Carnation, Clary Sage, Clove, Cumin, Galbanum, Geranium, Ginger, Hyssop, Juniper, Lavender, Lime, Melissa, Mimosa, Oak Moss, Palmarosa, Pimento Berry, Pine, Rosemary, Sage, Sweet Fennel, Tea-Tree, Thyme, Valerian, Violet, Yarrow
Day: Sunday
Astrology/Zodiac: Leo
Ascended masters with similar energy: Archeia Faith, El Morya, Apollo, Brighid, Horus, Krishna, Kuan Ti, Odin, Osiris, Pele
Egyptian name: Ra, Sekhmet and Re
Greek/Roman: God of Planet 'Helios,' Adonis/Sol, Apollo
Fixed stars (Leo): Regulus
Planet: The Sun

Archangel Raguel – Friend of God

Archangel Raguel's name means 'friend of God,' and he is often cited to as the 'Angel of Justice and Fairness.' Raguel is the angel to call upon to have harmonious relationships in our lives.

His energy brings all the qualities of equity, honesty, impartiality, objectiveness, rightfulness in your life. He can help us to see solutions that are realistic and achievable. Archangel Raguel is known for healing disagreements or misunderstandings; bringing harmony and peace to stressful situations; bringing in your life new friends who treat you with respect and integrity and keep that relationship in good terms. When Archangel Raguel is around you, you may see sparks, flashes or twinkles of pale blue light.

Angelic Ambassador of Harmony, Balance and Orderliness

Archangel Raguel is also known as the 'Angelic Ambassador of Harmony, Balance and Orderliness,' and the 'Divine Peacekeeper.' Archangel Raguel is recognized as the responsible for overseeing the other archangels and angelic beings, and guarantee that all is lining up with Divine order and Divine Laws. Raguel helps the planet bringing order and balance on Earthly matters; and the oppression that many of the populations and the planet can be suffering.

Angel of justice and legal matters

Raguel also works with similar energy of archangel Michael, being an angel of justice. He acts as a mediator in challenging and difficult situations to find a solution, always respecting the truth and divine order. He helps us to find peace and resolve situations that cause us stress. Raguel is an excellent helper in legal matters. Call upon him when you need assistance with any legal issue.

Mediation and harmony in relationships

Archangel Raguel assists bringing harmony within groups and families. He is a collaborator or mediator between two parts when there is not understanding, defending the unfairly treated, and bringing consensus in both sides. If you want to experience more harmonious relationships (of all kinds), and bring balanced, peaceful resolutions to disagreements or disputes, call upon archangel Raguel. He will guide you to find the best solutions respecting the highest good for all.

Bringing peace to the relationship with yourself

Archangel Raguel realigns you with your higher-selves, the divine truth, always respecting your integrity. If you are dealing with inner conflicts in your mind, spirit and body, you can call upon him to re-connect with the essence of who you really are. This act will empower you and your relationship. Raguel helps you to become your best friend, be in harmony with yourself and maintain this relationship even when you are dealing with difficult times in your life.

Managing chaos and stress

If any tension, crisis, stress or chaos arrives to your life, call upon archangel Raguel. He will assist you to choose more balanced perspectives, guiding you find inner-peace and harmony on these types of situations. Raguel reminds you that you are peace, and you can find peace in your heart. You cannot help the situation if you are on stress mode, but you can empower a situation if you choose peace. Peace is linked with experience faith and hope in the Divine order. Raguel is an excellent guide to help you to embrace these qualities.

Archangel Raguel works aligning and balancing the Root Chakra (first chakra) and Throat Chakra (fifth chakra). Work with him to manifest beautiful relationships, especially the feeling of belong to a tribe or group. And you can also call upon Raguel when working on speaking your inner truth, and/or being diplomatic in your speech.

Archangel Raquel is the patron angel of agriculture, community organizers, community planners, diplomats, farmers, industry, land owners, managers, manual laborers, mediators, multi-taskers, public speakers, social workers.

Archangel Raguel usually arrives in your life when it's time to organize priorities, when you need to bring peace to the relationship with yourself or others.

Archangel Raguel helps you:

* Finding resolutions
* Improving self-empowerment
* Creating opportunities on mediation and harmony in relationships
* Helping with legal matters
* Managing chaos and stress
* Experiencing peace with others and yourself
* Seeing things from a higher perspective
* Restoring balance and harmony

Also known as: Akrasiel, Raguil, Rasuil, Rufael, Suryan
Color: Pale blue
Crystal or gemstone: Aquamarine, Blue Lace Agate, Sodalite, Kyanite
Tarot Card: Justice

Focus: Harmony and relationships
Chakra: Root chakra (first chakra) and throat chakra (fifth chakra)
Trees: Bean, Hickory, Lucky Hand, Marigold, Pecan, Straw, Yerba Mate
Animals: Antelope, mouse, roadrunner, swift
Symbols: Books, quill and ink
Essential oils: Hickory
Day: Wednesday
Astrological / Zodiac: Sagittarius
Ascended Masters with the same energy: Lu-Hsing, Moses, Solomon
Planet: Mercury, Uranus

Archangel Raphael – God Heals

    The name Raphael means 'God heals,' 'God has healed,' 'Medicine of God,' derived from the Hebrew word 'Rapha' meaning 'healer' or 'doctor,' or 'Rapach', which means 'God heals the soul.' According to all Abrahamic religions, Raphael is the healing angel.

Raphael is related with the angel cited in the Gospel of John as rousing water at the healing pool of Bethesda. Raphael also accompanies Tobias, the son of Tobit and Sarah, on a journey to Medes on his father's behalf. Archangel Raphael heals Tobit of blindness, he also protects him during his journey and takes an evil out of Sarah. Raphael is one of the three angels who visited Abraham and his wife and helped them with the conception of his son. He also healed Abraham's grandson, Jacob. He is also the one who gave King Solomon his magical ring.

Archangel Raphael is the Archangel of the East ruling over the element of Air, and relates to the astrological signs of Gemini, Libra and Aquarius.

Archangel Raphael is the angel of healing for humans and animals, the angel of the soul mates, the angel that gives guidance and support to healers, helps with reducing and eliminating cravings and addictions, enhancing clairvoyance, retrieving lost pets, space clearing and traveling. The 'Divine healer,' has an energy of love, kindness, compassion, balance, inner-guidance and the capacity to heal ourselves and others. When Archangel Raphael is around you, you may see sparks, flashes or twinkles of emerald green light.

The doctor of the heaven

The celestial doctor is considered to be the patron of science and medicine, helping with inner and outer healing in all levels: mental, emotional, physical, spiritual. Archangel Raphael guides those who heal others, especially doctors, nurses, spiritual practitioners. He guides those who heal, prior to, and during treatment or healing sessions. He also helps aspiring healers with their education, then assists them with their healing practices.

Archangel Raphael is a powerful healer who works on releasing fear and shadows from your mind and body. He takes care of everything relating to the healing aspect including surgery to herbalism, from the personal to the planetary.

Archangel Raphael's energy can be called upon in any place of healing, including hospitals, hospices, healing rooms, etc. These energies can be called upon also to soften and heal the energies of nations in war and manmade and natural disasters. In addition, Raphael's energy can be called to guide scientists and researchers as they seek new cures for diseases.

You can call upon Archangel Raphael when you are dealing with physical challenges such as pain or when you are sick. He will comfort you soften and relieving your pain. Archangel Raphael brings healing with his beautiful emerald green healing energy and light.

If you or another person or animal are in physical pain, consider calling upon Archangel Raphael. He will act directly to bring you healing where you need.

Archangel Raphael also reminds us that forgiveness and unconditional love are the most powerful medicines to heal totally.

Breaking destructive cycles

Archangel Raphael helps us to dissolve any negative blockage caused by an addictive behavior or destructive cycle and which is causing us disease. He helps break these blockages; helping us to transform the lower energy into the positive power of love and manifesting healing in our lives.

Helping us to eliminate cravings and addictions

Archangel Raphael also helps if you are experiencing cravings and addictions by reducing and eliminating them, bringing balance and harmony to your life.

Encourage you to have a healthy lifestyle

You can also work with Raphael when you are starting a new healthy plan to improve the quality of your life, like a diet for example. Raphael encourages healthy eating and enjoyable exercise. He guides us to manifest positive changes to bring balance in the quality of your life. Call upon him in order to get the strength and motivation to follow a healthy plan.

Archangel of Science and Knowledge

If you are in the area of science investigation and research, call upon Archangel Raphael to get the inspiration and the connection to find and receive the information in these matters in order to help to heal others.

The angel of the blind

Archangel Raphael is the 'Angel of Truth and Vision.' Archangel Raphael heals Tobit of blindness and becomes the patron saint of the blind.

He also helps to open our soul eyes to see what we cannot see with our physical eyes.

The angel of the travelers

Because of Tobit's journey made in company of Raphael, he is considered 'the angel of the travelers.' You can ask Raphael for help with receiving collaboration from the airline, train or bus clerks; when you need assistance with your luggage or when you experience turbulence on your flight. You can call upon Raphael to assure that you stay well prior to and during your vacation, and to ensure a safe journey.

Helping you to find your soul mates

According to legend, St Raphael helped Tobias meet Sarah and married her. Until then, Sarah had no luck in marriage, with seven of her husband's finding unfortunate death. Raphael blessed the couple and protected them, so they could finally become pregnant and raise a family together.

Archangel Raphael is also the angel of the tarot card 'The Lovers,' reflecting a scene of blessing to Eve and Adam as the first couple on Earth. Raphael is the angel who watches over those who are seeking a soul mate.

Guiding your spiritual journey

Archangel Raphael helps those who dare to go on an internal spiritual journey, helping in their search for guidance and inner truth. Raphael is very connected to all light workers and assists them during their journey of self-discovery and when it's time to guide others looking for spiritual journeys.

Healing animals

Archangel Raphael assists the healing for both wild and domesticated animals, and also assists with finding lost pets. Call upon him, when you need assistance to heal your beloved pets or any animal in need of healing.

Archangel Raphael's spiritual retreat is over Fatima, Portugal, and you can visit there for healing and assistance to open your Heart Chakra. Archangel Raphael oversees the Heart Chakra helping you to understand unconditional love and knowing that love is the only medicine that heals your life. As that angel of the heart chakra, Raphael will guide you to heal your body, your mind, your heart; and help others to heal in divine order and divine time.

Archangel Raphael works with his twin flame, Lady Mary, mother of Jesus, the 'Queen of Angels,' overseeing the Fifth Ray, of Mind, Intellect and Healing. You can call upon the assistance of this ray, when you are looking for vision on your path, develop intuition and vision, concentration, focus, truth, for energies of nurturing, compassion, mercy and grace. Hilarion is the Chohan of the Green Ray of Mind, Intellect and Healing.

Archangel Raphael is the patron angel of astronomers, cartographers, doctors, healers, herbalists, intuitive people, lightworkers, the medical field, nurses, shamans and medicine women, stargazers, pilots, stewards, travelers.

Archangel Raphael usually arrives to your life when you need to heal your body, your mind or/and your heart. He also arrives in your life when you are starting your spiritual journey, or you need assistance on this journey. Raphael will show up in your life when you are meant to help to heal others.

Archangel Raphael helps you:

- Reducing and eliminating cravings and addictions
- Guiding you and protecting you while traveling
- Healing of body, mind, soul, and spirit
- Developing divine vision, intuition and insights
- Supporting to start and continue a healthy plan like a diet in your life
- Assisting to overcome healthy obstacles and addictions
- Assisting to heal animals
- Finding your soulmate
- Bringing inspiration for the study and practice of music, mathematics, science, and both traditional and alternative medicine

Also known as: Labbiel, Lord Raphael
Color: Emerald green
Crystal or gemstone: Emerald, Green Adventurine, Malachite, Green Fluorite, Chrysoprase
Tarot card: The lovers
Focus: Healing and harmony
Chakra: Heart chakra (fourth chakra)
Ray: The Fifth Ray, of Mind or Intellect
Element: Air
Direction: East

Trees: Hazel, Myrtle, Mulberry, Almond, Ash, Aspen, Bottle Brush, Hazel, Larch, Mulberry, Rowan, Silver Birch and Juniper
Animals: Cat, condor, eagle, deer, dolphin, dove, dragonfly, duck, frog, horse, owl, rabbit, snake, whale, wolf
Symbols: White feathers, the caduceus, eight pointed star
Essential oils: Star Anise, Lavender, Eucalyptus, Frankincense, Myrrh, Sage, Spearmint
Day: Wednesday
Astrology/Zodiac: Gemini
Ascended Masters with similar energy: Ishtar, Isis, Khonsu, Neptune, St. Padre Pio
Egyptian name: Thoth
Greek/Roman God of Planet: Hermes/Mercury
Fixed stars: Aldebaren, Rigel, Bellatrix, Capella and Polaris
Planet: Mercury

Archangel Raziel – Secrets of God

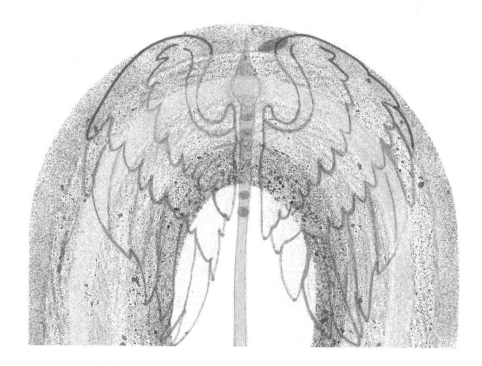

Archangel Raziel's name means 'secret of God.' It is said that he knows all the secrets and mysteries of the Universe and how it functions. Raziel is known in the Kabbalah as the 'Keeper of Secrets' and the 'Angel of Divine Mysteries.' He is associated with the Sephirah Chokhmah (the second of ten).

Raziel encourages us to strengthen our bonds to the spiritual realm and to operate the magic that exists in our hearts. When Archangel Raziel is around, you may see sparks, flashes or twinkles of rainbow light.

Helping us to develop our wisdom

Archangel Raziel's energy is similar to an old magician. His energy is mature and wise. Archangel Raziel's words are focused, intelligent, calm, and gentle. He has a lot of knowledge to share. When he is around pay careful attention to his message. He will also help you to develop your own wisdom and trust the message your heart is receiving from the heavens.

Renew your faith

Raziel is an excellent helper that will motivate you to restore and renew your faith. When you feel that you do not have any solution in your life, when you feel tired of trying and feel stuck where you are, call upon Raziel. He will help you to restore your faith in God or restore faith in yourself. He always has the answers you need in challenging situations.

Master of Divine information

Archangel Raziel is the Archangel of the 'Revelation of Divine Mysteries,' giving you the mysterious knowledge and divine wisdom on your path. Archangel Raziel is a spiritual guide and an esoteric master teacher for those who are on the spiritual path. Raziel helps you to connect with your intuition, so you can connect with the divine information that is available for all human beings at divine timing.

Raziel assists you to understand metaphysical and esoteric concepts. Archangel Raziel helps you with the principles of manifestation, alchemy, sacred geometry, quantum physics and other high-level information.

Archangel Raziel guides anyone on the esoteric and spiritual path. Call upon him, when you want to attend the celestial university and learn from a great master. He will teach you many aspects of metaphysics, numerology, astrology, astral travel, alchemy, chakras, crystals, energy healing, Reiki, shamanism and psychic development.

Enhance intuition and psychic gifts

Archangel Raziel helps to enhance intuition, clairvoyance, clairsentience, develop psychic abilities and spiritual wisdom. Call upon him when you need assistance to unblock, discover, and develop your divine gifts. Raziel will support you working with your divine tools, so you can help yourself and others; in divine order respecting the free will of everyone involved.

Divine communication

Archangel Raziel helps elevate self-awareness and understanding to develop your inner communication between your higher self and the divine helpers and guides. He will teach you to be aware and receptive to the celestial messages, so you can work together with your divine team; increasing your ability to hear, to know, to see and to feel.

Past-life issues

Archangel Raziel also helps with past life regressions. He also assists healing any trauma caused by past memories: especially of those that are blocking you to manifest your inner gifts and live your soul mission. Raziel helps to break any vow you may have done in a past life which is causing you an impediment in your current life. These vows can be related to: poverty, self-sacrifice, or chastity. Call upon him to break it down and be free to follow your soul's mission.

Magic and manifestation

Archangel Raziel is like the wizard and alchemist of the Archangels. He keeps the key to reveal all the secrets and mysteries of the Universe. Raziel is the Merlin of the heaven. He is covered by a radiant rainbow light. Through him find the magic of your heart through celestial rituals called 'Angel Magic.' (For more insight see Angel Magic: The Ancient Art of Summoning and Communicating with Angelic Beings by Geoffrey James, and very soon on my second book 'Walking with Angels II')

Call upon Raziel when you need to manifest any desire of your heart. There is only one important rule working with angels: Always respect the free will of everyone involved, the divine timing and the divine order. The rest will be orchestrated by the Universe with the assistance of Raziel.

Archangel Raziel is the patron angel of alchemy, computer science, cryptography, linguists, mathematics, magicians, metaphysics, mysteries, prophets, sacred geometry, scholars, secrets, the unknown, and visionaries.

Archangel Raziel usually arrives to your life when a revelation is to be imparted. This revelation will be helpful for your spiritual growth; or when you need to manifest your heart's desires in divine order and divine timing.

Archangel Raziel helps you:

- Enhancing intuition and psychic gifts
- Understanding metaphysical and esoteric aspects
- Developing self-awareness, self-knowledge and understanding
- Boosting knowledge and wisdom
- Manifesting your highest desires
- Healing painful memories
- Helping you to work on past-life regressions

- Assisting you in developing divine communication

Also known as: Ratziel, Saraqael, Suriel
Color: All the colors of the rainbow
Crystal or gemstone: Clear Quartz, Diamond, Smoky Quartz, Amethyst, Labrodite, Prehnite
Tarot card: The magician, The hermit
Focus: Intuition, spiritual insight and psychic abilities
Chakra: 3rd eye chakra, crown chakra
Element: Light
Trees: Belladonna, Eyebright, Garlic, Hemlock, Hickory
Animals: Chameleon, eel, fox, panther, raven, scorpion, snake, spider
Symbols: Blade/dagger, illuminated mind, keys, smoke, veil, mortar and pestle
Essential oils: Hickory, Ruda, Cinnamon
Day: Wednesday
Astrological/Zodiac: Leo
Ascended Master with similar energy: Merlin
Planet: Neptune

Archangel Sandalphon - Highest of Angels (twin)

Sandalphon and Metatron names end in 'on' instead of 'el'; which signifies his human origin. Sandalphon means 'brother' in Greek. He is said to be twin brother to Archangel Metatron. Sandalphon was the prophet Elijah, and Metatron was the wiseman Enoch. Besides the Kabbalah, both were humans and ascended into Angels. The Kabbalah mentions that Metatron presides over the entrance of the spheres of Tree of Life, and Sandalphon presides over its exit.

Sandalphon's functions include being the patron of musicians, helping determinate the gender of a child, being the carrier of prayers to God from humans. When Archangel Sandalphon is around you may see sparks, flashes or twinkles of rainbow turquoise.

The messenger of human prayers

Sandalphon is the energy link between man and spirit. He understands all human matters, due to his experience as a mortal one. He understands the power of prayer. He knows faith is necessary when we focus on our petitions, and that trusting in God is needed to receive answers from those prayers.

For human matters, Sandalphon is an excellent helper. He will understand, because he had once been in your shoes. Call upon him as your human friend in the heavens.

The Guardian of the Earth and the angel working with Pachamama

Archangel Sandalphon is the 'Guardian of the Earth' responsible for the progress and health of all the inhabitants of Earth. Sandalphon works on behalf of Pachamama (Mother Earth); in collaboration with all the elements of the planet (Air, Water, Earth, and Fire); and the Elemental realms (Elves, Gnomes, Fairies, Dryads, Brownies, Sylph, Mermaids, Undines, Salamanders, Djinns.) Sandalphon teaches us to connect and to work with these energies to bring harmony to our lives and peace to others' lives.

Earth healing

Archangel Sandalphon is the angel of earth healing and distance healing. Archangel Sandalphon guides all those who are working on the environment and healing our planet. He is also an excellent guide when you want to send healing to others in the world, as well as those who are suffering wars and catastrophes around the globe.

The angel of grounding and connection to your roots

Archangel Sandalphon helps you to integrate healing energy within the physical body, so you can maintain balance in your life. He is an excellent helper to work on grounding as a spiritual practice; connecting yourself to this planet and the elementals of the trees, plants, flowers and crystals.

Sandalphon guides you to connect with your roots, helping you to correlate with your ancestors and the place you were born in this life. If you are far from your place of birth, call upon Sandalphon to feel connected with the land where your life originated. Sandalphon is a wonderful guide to shamanic practices.

Angel of Music and Prayer

Archangel Sandalphon is known as the 'Angel of Music.' Music is a powerful mechanism to boost, develop and sustain a positive vibration and mental state. Call upon Archangel Sandalphon to develop your musical skills and guide you towards a career or training involving music as part of your soul path. Sandalphon can also guide and oversee your career path within the music industry.

Archangel Sandalphon will assist Archangel Uriel working on our Root chakra. Together they help us to ground ourselves; to feel safe and secure; and to focus on the place we live now: planet Earth.

Archangel Sandalphon is the patron angel of academics, musicians, children with disabilities, concentration, florists, gifts, charity, the homeless, midwives, music, playfulness and games, prayer, puzzles, riddles, secrets, school exams, unborn children, youth.

Archangel Sandalphon usually arrives in your life when you need to ground yourself and connect to your roots. Establishing the link with your own roots will help you discover a life of perfect harmony.

Archangel Sandalphon helps you with:

- Stability, balance and freedom
- Assistance in your prayers
- Any human aspect request
- Healing Mother Earth
- To ground and connect with your ancestors
- Integrating healing energy within the physical body
- Musical skills and career

Also known as: Sandalphon, Sandalfon
Color: Turquoise
Crystal or gemstone: Turquoise, Amazonite, Apatite, Aquamarine, Blue Tourmaline
Tarot Card: The hierophant
Focus: Environmental awareness, personal and global responsibility
Chakra: Earth star (situated below the feet)
Trees: Blueberry, Gardenia, Lemon, Lemon Balm, Lemongrass, Lettuce, Magnolia, Moss, Passion Flower, Pineapple, Raspberry, Rhubarb, Strawberry, Sugarcane, Sweet Pea, Tulip, Violet

Animals: Canary, coyote, dog, otter, porcupine
Symbols: Harp, wrapped presents
Essential oils: Citrus, Blueberry, Gardenia, Pineapple, Sandalwood, Strawberry
Day: Friday
Ascended masters with similar energy: Cherubs, Cupid, Damara, elves and fairies, Hathor, John the Baptist, Kwan Yin, St. Theresa
Planet: Venus

Archangel Uriel – Light of God

Archangel Uriel means 'Fire of God,' 'Flame of God,' 'Light of God,' 'God's Light,' 'God is Light,' 'Radiation of God.' His primary mission is to enlightenment allowing us to focus on our strengths and strengthen our weak areas. Being the angel of Earth, Uriel teaches us to connect with our planet. Uriel brings harmony and world peace. He is the angel that illuminates our minds with information, ideas and insights. When you are looking for an answer, he will whisper it to you. Call upon Archangel Uriel when you need a solution for business matters, when you need assistance while writing, while studying or taking a test. When Archangel Uriel is around, you may see sparks, flashes or twinkles of red and gold light.

Elevate your soul and spirituality

Uriel's energy is bright and powerful, enlightening your soul and spirit to connect with the divinity. Uriel can help you achieve your higher calling by aligning you to high vibrations. In your spiritual practices, call upon him while you focus on your solar plexus chakra and visualize the sun irradiating light from this place to the rest of your body. Then visualize this light covering all your aura and helping you to elevate to the higher realms.

Angel of light and vitality

Archangel Uriel is associated with light, electricity, lightning, courage, vitality and fortitude. Archangel Uriel revitalizes you while activate and increase the energy
in your body's system. If you feel you are lacking energy and stamina, call upon Archangel Uriel to boost you and inject your body with vitality.

Helping to manifest

As the angel of Earth, Uriel can teach you to work in the practice to manifest to physical level what is in your mind, thus materializing the desires of your heart. If you are working with the law of attraction, call upon Archangel Uriel to help you to manifest what is vibrating in your inner higher self.

Angel of peace

Archangel Uriel is the 'Angel of Peace,' or the 'Archangel of Divine Peace'. He is represented holding a flame: meaning that he offers the 'Flame of Love' towards all souls.
Archangel Uriel brings inner peace to anyone in this planet. Call upon Uriel when you want to irradiate peace on a situation or when you need

help to resolve dilemmas.

Angel of salvation

Being known as the 'Angel of Salvation,' Archangel Uriel can help you to find grace in any challenge. He can help you grow and evolve as you see the lessons and gifts in any difficult situation. Uriel shows that you can save yourself and be that hero you were looking for. Uriel can guide you to connect with the inner savior within you.

Divine plan and karma

Uriel helps you to understand the concept of the Universal Spiritual Law of Karma (Cause and Effect). Uriel helps you to understand that everything happening in your life, is in divine order and planed perfectly to achieve the lessons your soul needs to reach out in this lifetime. He motivates you to trust on this divine and perfect plan, so you can embrace and understand all the blessings behind any challenging situation.

Prophecies and warnings

Archangel Uriel is the angel that interprets prophecies, coming to you through your intuition and dreams. Uriel helps you to find the light in those messages, so you can download the information and apply it to your life. During your night ritual, add a prayer to Uriel to help you to understand those important messages on a conscious level.

Cleansing

Archangel Uriel spreads transformative energies to the mind, cleansing your thoughts. Uriel can bring light to those thoughts that are not helping us to evolve as soul beings. Call upon Archangel Uriel when you want to work with positive affirmations and visualizations, in order to achieve your heart's desires.

Clarity and insight

Archangel Uriel can be invoked for clarity and insight. We can envision and understand situations in life following the divine gift of our intuition. Call upon Uriel, when you need assistance in clarifying your ideas and bring answers to resolve any issue you may be going through.

Releasing fears

Archangel Uriel helps you to release your fears and connect with your higher wisdom. Archangel Uriel brings the light to your inner self; so, you can find courage to pursue your life purpose and the happiness you deserve. He assists with the development of self-confidence and self-worth.

With this light in you, you can dissipate the fears and illusions that block you to advance on your path of life.

Discover life purpose

Archangel Uriel helps you to discover your life path. Illuminating your inner being. Uriel is able to bring light to those dark areas at which you are afraid to look. Sometimes your inner gifts are hidden on those places, and you need the courage to go and look for it. Archangel Uriel is your guide on this quest. He will coach you to discover those inner gifts, so you can embrace your life purpose.

Helping to focus and using your intellect

Archangel Uriel brings practical solutions: wisdom and knowledge, vision, understanding and enlightened knowledge. Call upon Uriel to boost your ideas and insight to pursuit your academic challenges such as tests and exams.

Weather concerns

Archangel Uriel is the archangel to called when you are afraid for weather issues. He is associated with thunder and lightning. Uriel helps us during natural disasters and Earth changes as: earthquakes, fires, floods, tornadoes, hurricanes. He can be called during extreme weather conditions, and to recover from these natural events.

Archangel Uriel is the archangel of the north, ruling over the element of Earth, and relates to the astrological signs of Taurus, Virgo and Capricorn.

Archangel Uriel's spiritual retreat is over the Tatra Mountains in Poland. If you visit there, you can ask for relief and healing of fears and doubts, and to increase the flame of peace within you and the planet.

Archangel Uriel and his twin flame Aurora, work on the 'Ruby Ray,' the Sixth Ray of Devotion, allowing humanity to connect to their soul's wisdom.

On a chakra level, archangel Uriel oversees the Root chakra helping us to connect with our roots, our ancestors, our tribe, our family and of course this planet that is our home: planet Earth.

Archangel Uriel is the patron angel of judges, lawmakers, peacemakers, prophets, seekers of truth, missionaries, ministers, priests, nuns, nurses, caregivers, healers, physicians, social workers, community workers, lawyers, farmers and teachers.

Archangel Uriel usually arrives to your life when you are going to pursuit a path of a scholar, a teacher or a prophet. He also arrives to your life to bring illumination on any aspect of your life pushing you to be aligned with your soul purpose.

Archangel Uriel helps you with:

- Achieving goals and aspirations
- Elevating your soul and spirituality
- Vitalizing your physical body
- Helping to manifest your heart's desires
- Bringing peace in challenging situations in your life
- Bringing peace in your heart
- Finding practical solutions
- Helping you to be responsible for your acts
- Helping you to understand karmic lessons
- Clarity, insight, and understanding
- Releasing energy blocks
- Releasing fears and traumas
- Helping to understand prophecies and messages through dreams
- Cleaning your thoughts and improve positive affirmations
- Discover your life purpose

Other names: Auriel
Color: Ruby and gold
Crystal or gemstone: Hematite, Obsidian, Ruby, Rutilated Quartz, Tiger's Eye, Citrine
Tarot card: The Sun
Focus: Spiritual devotion through selfless service to humanity, ideas and intelligence
Chakra: Root or base chakra (first chakra)
Ray: The Sixth Ray, of Devotion
Element: Earth

Direction: North
Trees: Ash, Basil, Black Pepper, Bloodroot, Cactus, Chili Pepper, Cinnamon, Clove, Cumin, Curry, Fig, Garlic, Hops, Horseradish, Juniper, Leek, Mistletoe, Nettle, Nutmeg, Peppermint, Radish, Rosemary, Sandalwood, Snapdragon,Thistle
Animals: Boar, lizard, phoenix, rhinoceros, snow leopard
Symbols: The flame of love, glyph, made of flames
Essential oils: Cinnamon, Nutmeg, Sandalwood
Day: Thursday
Astrology/Zodiac: Aquarius
Ascended Masters with similar energy: Forseti, Idaten, Lilith, Maat, Thor
Planet: Uranus

Archangel Zadkiel – Righteousness of God

Archangel Zadkiel's name means 'the righteousness of God,' 'the Justice of God,' 'Knowledge of God.' Archangel Zadkiel is also known as the 'Holy One,' the 'Angel of Mercy,' the 'Angel of Understanding and Compassion,' and the Archangel of 'Divine Joy.' Zadkiel helps us with forgiveness and compassion, experience love within us, and to love others as God loves us. He can also help you heal emotional pain from your past. He gives us strength to confront our wounds, reminds us to be grateful and be thankful for all the love in our lives.

In Jewish rabbinical writings, Zadkiel is cited as the archangel who encourages forgiveness and compassion in people. In the Kabbalah, Zadkiel presides over the fourth Sephirah on the Tree of Life helping us to practice unconditional love on Earth.

His energy is pleasant, soft, profound and inspirational. His words are always calm and tender. When Archangel Zadkiel is around you, you may see sparks, flashes or twinkles of violet or dark purple light.

The angel of forgiveness

Archangel Zadkiel encourages you to understand others, accepting them as they are and not as you expect them to be. He helps you to realize that forgiveness is a gift from your heart, knowing that it's not important who is right or who is wrong. Zadkiel teaches you that forgiveness releases a huge emotional weight from your heart; setting you free and clearing space in your heart to feel love. You can call on him when you need help with forgiveness; whether it's forgiving yourself, asking forgiveness from God, or forgiving someone else.

The angel of the Violet Flame and Transmutation

Archangel Zadkiel rules the highest vibration in the rainbow, the Violet Ray which is the 7th ray of the rainbow's color spectrum. Archangel Zadkiel is the keeper of the Violet Flame and he is called on to transmute negative energies. Using the Violet Flame, Archangel Zadkiel frees us from the energy of any challenging situation. He helps us to develop psychic abilities, understanding our dreams, and enhancing intuition.

Zadkiel helps you to understand the purpose of difficult situations in your life, so you can overcome them and grow from those lessons. Archangel Zadkiel holds your energy and transforms it with the power of the Violet Flame transmuting any negative energy into joy, compassion and peace.

Angel of freedom and mercy

Archangel Zadkiel is the archangel of freedom and mercy. He teaches you that you can achieve freedom when you liberate yourself from anger, resentment, and any lower energy feeling through forgiveness. Zadkiel teaches you to raise your energies, by being thankful for small and big blessings in your lives. When we achieve this state of gratitude, we can resonate with balance, calmness and peace. It's in this state where we experience the freedom of our soul.

Helping with memory

Archangel Zadkiel is known for helping us with our memory. Zadkiel helps students remember details, information and data for tests. Call upon him, when you need a boost in your recall especially for tests, important meetings or interviews.

Healing form painful past memories

Archangel Zadkiel brings healing to emotional distress caused by hurtful memories from the past. Using forgiveness as a tool of healing, Zadkiel can repair a broken heart spreading compassion and unconditional love to the hurtful memory. He also helps you reconnect with those beautiful moments of your life, teaching you that life has blessings and challenges and that you are more than those memories of the past. He helps you to change your perspective: from a victim role to a creator role, the role of the hero.

Archangel Zadkiel also helps to heal from painful memories of past lives. He is an excellent guide to practitioners of past life regressions, Akashic records readers, and any practice which includes healing past life issues. Call upon him when you know your pain is not from this life. He will help you identify that painful memory and to bring peace to that past life situation.

Teaching self-love and self-acceptance

Archangel Zadkiel teaches you unconditional love reminding you that this starts with yourself. He is a wonderful life coach to guide you on the process of accepting yourself as you are, and not as society or others would want. Zadkiel focus on lightening your unique skills and inner gifts so you can really know yourself and see the unique beauty that resides within you. The more you can see and reconnect, the more you will embrace your soul path and your life purpose, and the more you will be in alignment with life.

Divine knowledge and spiritual awakening

Archangel Zadkiel assists with spiritual awakenings, awareness and soul evolution. Archangel Zadkiel is associated with Universal Divine knowledge and wisdom; guiding all human being on their spiritual path. This angelic guide supports any person looking for divine connection to understand their soul map. He assists those who are questioning themselves about the role of their existence; supporting the big wave of spiritual awakenings, we are going through nowadays. Call upon him when you need to get in touch with divine wisdom and when you need a partner on this process.

Helping to free ourselves from karmic contracts

Archangel Zadkiel helps you to free yourself from karmic blockages and contracts. Zadkiel helps you to see yourself and others with love and compassion, helps you understand the importance of those contracts to close the cycle and to finally break these contracts. Zadkiel helps you realize that you cannot escape from those contracts. Once you understand the lesson and the responsibility, you can take actions to close those circles and let them go with unconditional love.

Archangel Zadkiel and his twin flame Holy Amethyst have their etheric retreat, known as the 'Temple of Purification', over the island of Cuba. Visit this retreat to learn the true meaning of spiritual freedom, transmutation through forgiveness, mercy and compassion.

As said before, Archangel Zadkiel is the angel of the Violet Flame and the Seventh Ray of Freedom and Ceremonial Magic, helping humanity to understand that freedom can only be possible with forgiveness and the magic of unconditional love. It's at this moment that your soul can experience peace and harmony.

Archangel Zadkiel oversees the Crown Chakra (seventh chakra) which supports us connecting with higher realms and our higher inner being, as well as helping us to recognize that we are all gods and goddesses of a unique universe: your own being.

Archangel Zadkiel is associated with the Ascended Master Saint Germain, who is the patron angel of academics, charity groups, ministers, diplomats, philanthropists, places of worship, prisoners, saints, students, visionaries, mystics, community organizers and those who assist others.

Archangel Zadkiel usually arrives to your life when you need to reexamine your life and focus on forgiving yourself and others.

Archangel Zadkiel helps you:

- Overcoming any challenging situation
- Teaching you to forgive yourself and others

- Experiencing freedom of the soul
- Helping you with your memory
- Healing painful memories from the past
- Developing and strengthening intuition
- Remembering your divine gifts and your life purpose
- Forgiving others and yourself
- Being grateful for any blessing in your life including the challenging lessons
- Overcoming obstacles
- Increasing your self-esteem
- Guiding spiritual awakenings
- Helping to free yourself from karmic contracts
- Transforming past memories, limitations and addictions
- Serving others and your soul mission

Also known as: Tzadkiel, Tzaphqiel, Tzaphquiel, Tzaphkiel, Hesediel, Jafkiel, Japhkiel, Satquiel, Satqiel, Zachiel, Zadakiel, Zadkiel, Zafkiel, Zaphiel, Zafchial, Zaphkiel, Zedekiel, Zedkiel, Zidekiel
Color: Violet & Lilac
Crystal or gemstone: Amethyst, Crystal Quartz, Jade, Kunzite, Ametrine, Blue Chalcedony, Tanzanite, Charoite, Fluorite
Tarot card: Temperance
Focus: Self-transformation, compassion and forgiveness, accessing angelic guidance
Chakra: Crown chakra
Ray: The Seventh Ray, of Freedom and Ceremonial Magic
Element: Cosmic energy
Trees: Oak, Ash, Cedar, Clive, Peach, Pecan, Rosemary, Oak
Animals: Elephants, whales, swans, ducks, dove, goat, sheep
Symbols: Books, scroll, shepherd's crook
Essential oil: Benzoin, Peach, Rosemary
Day: Saturday
Astrology/Zodiac: Pisces, Sagittarius
Ascended master with similar energy: Manjushri, Melchizedek, Nabu
Planet: Saturn

CHAPTER 4: COMMUNICATING WITH ANGELS AND ARCHANGELS

Learning to talk with the angels is similar to talk with ourselves, but in a deep way that allows us to connect strongly with our divine helpers. Learning to communicate with them opens the gate of interrelation with the Universe, and this helps us to start our role of co-creators of our own lives.

Everyone has the ability to communicate with angels. You just need to follow some values and add spiritual practices in your daily life. What we really communicate is: what we are, what we feel, and not so much what we can speak with words.

Developing certain attitudes towards life, towards people, towards animals, toward the planet, and of course towards ourselves, help us to be attuned to celestial messages. The first thing to consider is that we need to believe and trust in your angelic guides in order to keep active the channels of communication. If we do not trust or believe, the connection will not happen. Keep in mind that we need to be like little children, always keeping the faith. This is crucial for any connection you may want to establish on the spiritual realm.

The angels are our friends, our allies. In your daily life, you entertain a relationship with your friends. You call them, you visit them, you are constantly trying to get to them to spend time together and communicate with them as much as you can. The same thing applies to your celestial team. Talk to them, not only to ask them favors, but to tell them about your day, to thank them for any small or big blessing of your day, to tell them what is happening in your life. This attitude will strength your connection with them.

Another attitude necessary to get them closer to you, is to be transparent, to live your truth. Being transparent and coherent requires a lot of strength because society teaches to be opaque. However, living your truth implies commitment with your role as a lightworker. For example, if I am talking all the time about unconditional love and having some difficulties in my family on this topic or I do not have a good relationship with my husband/wife/girlfriend/boyfriend, etc., everything I am doing is fake. We are not honoring our truth with our actions. And that's the most important key at the time to establish connection with angels, archangels, and any kind of spiritual guidance from the Etheric plane. Remember, you can lie to them, but you can NOT lie to God/The Supreme Source or yourself!

Angels and heavenly spirits only ask us to live what we are, so we can be able to open those channels of communication. And I believe that if you are reading this book, it's because you are able to open a celestial door and connect with angels.

Gratitude is another quality that raises our energy to the celestial vibration. When you focus on blessings, you raise your energy and you open a door to establish contact with them. Try to think on all the blessings of your life or your day, before starting to connect with angels. You will see the results very quick.

Once you reach this level of connection, the angels will communicate the message in a direct way, nonverbal way. They can speak from inside or outside, sending you messages or signs on the outside world or within you. Sometimes you cannot understand the words but be sure your heart will feel and process on a soul level. Just open your heart and surrender to their lovely advice on divine time and divine order.

How to entertain a relationship with your angels?

Angels contact everyone who wants to establish a relationship with them. They do not choose 'important' people or 'gifted' people. They are opened to communicate with everyone who is willing to believe and to trust. They are very joyful beings. Behaving like a little child, bringing a pure heart, faith, good humor, facilitates the connection with angels. They love high vibration music, plants, fragrances, and kids.

Do not think you need to create a mysterious ritual in a dark room full of candles. You can talk to them anytime, anyplace; so, go ahead and start to establish this heavenly relationship.

Ask your angels about any issue you that triggers you. Open your heart, connect with them and accept the answer they bring to you. You need to trust that this answer will come into your life at the right time, and at the right moment. Angels do not have the same concept of time that we have as humans. They respect a divine plan and your soul plan as well. These answers can arrive to you in many ways: dreams, signs, people that can give you the answers, the TV, a song, a book.

Just trust and accept that your soul has a plan strictly respected by all your angels and spiritual helpers. We always get the answers we are looking for, just trust!! For sure, they will do their job.

Angels and symbols

Angels are spiritual beings having a higher frequency than humans. These supernatural beings know the truth of us as whole, complete and perfect and are always striving for our good. Their purpose is to help us to achieve happiness while we evolve during our soul adventure in a human body. They want you to follow and live your life purpose!

When you increase your awareness related to them, you will notice their guidance and support. Their guidance can come on different ways to your life and different forms of channeled messages, insights, signs, clues, and dreams, during your meditation or spiritual practices. The angels also can guide you through synchronicities: the 'casual' chain of significant events that come to your path to help you to follow your soul mission; while respecting the highest good and the sacred order of the cosmos.

Remember that every day represents an opportunity for you to pay attention to the language of the heaven. Take signs and symbols as a game, embracing it with a lot of fun and gratitude.

Feathers

When angels want you to know that you have been visited by them, they send feathers on your way, especially white ones. You can collect those feathers that you found and put them in on a box or shelf in your angelic altar. You can carry or wear the feather during the day and give them gratitude for their assistance. Know that they are with us all the time.

Angel shapes

You can find shapes in clouds in the sky, in bubbles in your bath, the shape of the water in your tea or coffee. Keep your eyes opened, they are trying to tell you that they are always supporting you.

Rainbows

When you see a rainbow, you feel blessed. The angels show on the material world that magic can happen anytime, and that you are surrounded by them. Have you ever seen that face of a child when he/she sees a rainbow? Magic opens for the little ones and those who believe. Time to believe!

Pennies

Angels often leave coins on our path as a symbol of prosperity support. If you see a penny on the ground, do not hesitate and pick it up. Abundance in all forms is arriving to your life.

Gather all the pennies you find and put them in a special box for abundance. Anytime you feel worried about money issues, go to your box and remember that you are prosperous on an etheric level.

Angel Numbers

One of my favorite ways to receive messages is through angel numbers. Angels are always trying to communicate with us by numbers and their sequences.

You will notice you are receiving this kind of sign when you watch your clock and see a sequence of numbers, when you see numbers: on the TV, a billboard, on a car tag, or even phone numbers or numbers of an address.

There are many books just focused on this subject. If you feel, you want to go deeper and learn more, see the 'Recommended readings' section.

Different numeric sequences have different meanings. Here are there is a brief meaning of the most common angel numbers:

Number 111: This angel number has a strong energy blueprint. New doors and opportunities are opening for you; and those favorable circumstances are aligning with your dreams and desires. Time to manifest what it's in your heart and to create blessings in your life. Stay calm and positive, pay attention to your thoughts to attune their energy with the Law of Attraction. Time to create what you have been holding in your deep inner self for long time.

Number 222: Keep holding positive thoughts. This number has to do with manifestation, keeping in balance, and creating blessings. You are planting seeds for a substantial harvest in the future. Yes! It's a confirmation you are walking in the right direction. Choices are opening for you. Stay positive, know that your angels are supporting and guiding you. However, always in mind to ask for their assistance, especially when you need to make important decisions in your life.

Number 333: You are open to spiritual experiences. The Ascended Masters and spiritual guides are answering your prayers and ready to work with you. Time to call for assistance to this incredible time to awaken and develop your spiritual gifts and psychic abilities. Jesus, Moses, Mary, Quan Yin, and Yogananda are some of the masters that can connect with you. Start to work with the energy that resonate in your heart. Open your heart, feel and hear the messages. You are growing on this sacred path!

Number 444: The angels are with you! You are not alone in this journey. You have never been alone. Your celestial team is working close to you, supporting you, embracing every take you take and helping you. Remember to listen your intuition; the more you connect with yourself, the more you will be connected to the angelic realm. Close your eyes and feel their presence, feel their wings hugging you, comforting you, supporting you. They are here now!

Number 555: The angels want you to be ready to embrace change in your life. Even if a transition seems to be complicated, there is always a gift of deep learning for your soul. Embrace the richness and the lessons of this transition, this only a great opportunity for your soul. The angels will be there to help you to go through this challenging time. Everything is going to be ok. Just trust on the divine plan and enjoy the change.

Number 666: This is a spiritual wakeup call from your angels. They want to let you know you have been focused on material matters and ignoring your inner voice and spiritual path. Listen to your heart instead of your head. Come back to the source of you: your soul. Get out of your noisy daily life and connect with yourself and the Creator. The only way you can balance your life is going inside of you. Do not look outside. All the answers are already in.

Number 777: Congratulations, miracles are around the corner, and you will receive it soon in your life. You and your celestial team are working together to manifest divine magic. Listen to the Divine and your inner self. You are on the right path to receive a reward for your spiritual work dedication.

Number 888: This is the angel number of abundance reminding that you have access to the infinite prosperity of the Universe. Angels helps you with abundance and abundance in any area of our life, like romance, career or health. Embrace this state of balance with the Universe, as you receive messages for your life purpose, goals and dreams. The Creator wants to compensate you for sharing your gifts with others. Open your arms to receive and be ready to stay open to any kind of abundance, even the ones coming on an unexpected way.

Number 999: Everything has a beginning and an end. Life is "cyclical," and number 9 shows us that a cycle is ending soon. Cycles are part of the Nature. As the planet goes through many cycles, we do the same. This phase of your life is about to be completed. Time to enjoy the results of the hard work you put into it and time to start creating a new cycle on your life.

Number 000: A reminder that you are one with God. Feel the unity with everything that surround you, because everything and everyone are God as well.

Fragrances

Angels love fragrances and they are essential when you want to make connection with angels. Angels love nature, plants, and flowers, and can make their appearances through the power of smell. They love to pull your attention when from nowhere, you smell a very familiar aroma. At this moment, feel their presence and their love.

Sparkles of light

Angels love to play with the whole spectrum of colors. Sometimes they choose to appear in your presence showing flashes of colors and shimmers of light. Remember that each angel has their specific color. When you feel sparkles of light, start to familiarize with the angel who is contacting you by their own colors. Enjoy those encounters.

Contacting you in your dreams

Angels often come to us while we sleep: taking advantage that our consciousness is resting. The unconsciousness is more receptive to the heavenly messages given by our angels and spiritual guides. A good practice is to ask advice of your angels before going to sleep, and trust that you will receive that answer you are looking for. When you wake up, be ready to write down those messages as soon as you can. We start to lose track of our dreams as we advance during our day. For this practice, keep a dream journal close to your bed where you record all dream communication with your angels.

Hearing angelic voices

Angels sometimes try to communicate with us whispering slowly in our ears. When you hear them, do not question it. Just relax and receive with gratitude the message. You will probably take a couple of days to process that message and start to apply it in your life little by little.

Magazines or Books

If a book or a magazine suddenly falls from a shelf, then you need to pay attention. Open the book and do not hesitate, read the first paragraph you see. Remember, angels are always trying to connect with you and help you on your path.

Sensations and change in temperature

You might get goose bumps or tingling at the back of your neck or head because of the change of temperature that can indicate the presence of angels in the room.

They can show up to you through different kind of sensations. You will notice as soon as they are stimulating your body terminals.

Babies

Babies are such pure beings and remind us about the beauty of our souls. Angels love to be around babies due to their clear and soft energy. If you see a baby smiling at you when you were looking for a sign of love, be sure the angels are around that moment telling you that they love you and support you on your path.

People as messengers of the heaven

Sometimes angels can take the throat chakra of another person to give you a message. This person can be or not be known by you and can tell you the answer you were looking for to receive. Just pay attention to all the little gifts you can have in all the encounters in your daily life. You will be surprised how many messages you receive per day.

Advertisements or billboards

The angels can show you angel numbers, or simply the message you are looking forward to receive on a billboard or an advertisement. It's an easy way for them to pass messages to us due to our human routines. Open your eyes and your heart to receive those angelic messages.

CHAPTER 5: ANGELS AND ESSENTIALS OILS

For centuries, different cultures have used the qualities of essential oils to improve psychical, mental and spiritual well-being. Much data left from ancestral cultures include the therapeutical use of essential oils on healing practices. Essential oils are powerful tools assisting with angelic communication, spiritual practices including meditation, yoga, or just honor your sacred space during your spiritual practices.

Essential oils are extremely complex, on average most essential oils contain over 100 components including phenols, esters, aldehydes, ketones, alcohols, and terpenes. The combination of two or more essential oils creates a new fusion.

Essential oils are pure extracts from flowers, herbs, leaves, roots, and other plant parts. Essential oils bring the higher vibration and energy of the plant and their parts.

Each essential oils has a unique vibration. Most of them carry a high frequency. You can enjoy this divine and rooted vibration just by smelling or rubbing on your skin. This simple act will help you to align your vibration with the angel vibration.

Regarding the angels, they love to work with essential oils due to the connection with the power of nature. We can use many kinds of essential oils to connect with the healing powers of both: the elements of the plant and the help of the archangels. Essential oils are associated to archangels to address any issues and problems in our lives.

On the following lines, I provide advice how to use some essential oils to strengthen the connection with your Archangels during the healing of a specific issue. However, if you feel your intuition is telling you to add or to change any fragrance, please follow what your heart is communicating to you. There is not strict rule at when combining the essential oils, so please use your intuition.

How to use Essential Oils

There are several methods of using essential oils in your sacred space. Choose what is best for you:

- Diffuser: Put few drops of essential oils in the diffuser
- Water bowl: fill a small bowl with boiling water and add few drops of essential oil
- Candles: Add few drops of essential oil on the wax, not on the wick
- Room sprays: Fill a small bottle of spry with water and add ten drops of essential oil. Then spray the room
- Pillows: Sprinkle two drops of essential oil on the pillow in the sacred space that you use for meditation, therapy, and angelic exercises
- Incense or smudge sticks: Add three drops of essential oils to incense or smudge stick
- Hands: Put one drop pf essential oil on to the palm of one of your hands or your wrist

Essential Oils that empower your connection with angels

Angelica: This oil helps you to align your energies to the angelic realm. When you need a boost to connect with your celestial team or when you want to dispel fears and feelings of uncertainty, use Angelica oil. It will assist you with angelical connection.

Basil: This oil will help you to clear the mind and promotes clear thinking. It will help you to sooth your mind to be ready to receive important messages with no judgement; accepting the information as a gift of God.

Bay: This oil will encourage you to let go the past and all the negativity that carried in your present life. Bay also promotes enthusiasm for the future. This essential oil is associated with changing and moving on.

Black Pepper: This essential oil is very helpful for protection, and it also works align with the angels of protection.

Cardamom: This oil assists you when you need to establish a connection and balance with the three main aspects of your being: body, mind, and soul.

Carrot seed: This essential oil is used for opening the third eye and giving us visions and insight. It helps us to establish angelic connection and communication.

Cedarwood: This essential oil is very helpful when you need to uplift your energies and tap into your inner wisdom, so you can start to tune on the angelic realm. This is the oil of the wise ones.

Chamomile: This oil has the quality to bring inner peace and joyfulness into your present moment. Also, aids during meditation and promote a restful sleep.

Cinnamon: This essential oil is an excellent attractor. If you want to attract more beauty in your life, start to work with this oil. Cinnamon also helps us when we need to concentrate by stimulating mental powers. Use it when you need to work with the Law of Attraction.

Clary Sage: This oil helps you to clear away inner conflict and clean lower energies from places. It's very helpful to bring harmony and purpose in your life.

Coriander: If you are going through a personal change in your life, and you need angelic assistance to support you on this transition, use this essential oil.

Cypress: This essential oil can be used to help you to deal with grief and sorrow. Call upon archangel Azrael to support you on this chapter using cypress to help you to accept and let go.

Eucalyptus: This essential oil is excellent to use during healing rituals and to clear negative energy away. Very helpful when you call upon Raphael for healing intentions.

Frankincense: This is one of the essential oils that brings high spiritual vibration. In Biblical times it was considered one of the most valuable anointing oils. It was also one of baby Jesus's gifts brought by the Magic Kings. It will help you to prepare yourself and the environment energetically to lift the vibration to connect with your angels.

Geranium: This essential oil helps you to open your heart to connect with the angelic realm. It aids to balance and calms your emotions while you open your intuition.

Hyssop: This essential oil is excellent at the moment of clearing spaces, purifying them and repelling negative energies. When you have a clear space is easier to establish angelic connection. Hyssop promotes inner peace, balance, gratitude, forgiveness and faith; essential values aligned with the angelic vibration.

Jasmine: This essential oil helps us to open consciousness and awareness. You can use it to start your meditations to connect with your angelic team.

Juniper: This essential oil helps us to clear energies. It is used to purify and protect people and places. Juniper aids also to clear past traumas.

Lavender: Lavender has so many beneficial properties. This essential oil is used for protection and promotes inner harmony and compassion. Lavender aids you to relax your busy mind and calms you down so you can begin angel communication.

It's very helpful to enhance your psychic abilities, specially related with your third eye opening. It will be very favorable at the moment of connection with your angels and spiritual guides.

Lemon: This essential oil helps you to bring balance and sharpens your mind. It helps to focus your attention and your energies on your intention. It also brings the light of the sun and the joy, that are essential at the moment of connection with your angels.

Linden blossom: This essential oil is a basic heavenly essence. It connects us to the open our heart chakra and brings us a feeling of peace, love, forgiveness, and healing.

Marjoram: This essential oil is used to open the Heart Chakra and align yourself with the feeling of compassion, forgiveness, and unconditional love.

Melissa: This essential oil has the ability to draw angelic energy filling our hearts with joy and peace. This oil uplifts our souls to a spiritual level acting as a bridge between the earth and the heaven.

Myrrh: This oil was also one of the gifts for baby Jesus brought by the Magic Kings. It helps to purify our energy. Myrrh helps you to connect with higher energies and of course the angelic realm. You can use it also to release any blockage from past traumas.

Neroli: This essential oil has the ability to fill our body, mind and spirit with light. It helps us to find the answers that we are looking for and moving forward in our lives.

Orange: This essential oil can be used on your angelic altar to promote their presence in our space. Orange uplift our spirits and enhances our vital energy.

Peppermint: This essential oil clears your mind and refreshes our environment creating a perfect space to start our meditation or spiritual practices. The aroma of peppermint removes any blockage, so we can be able to receive the love of the angels and connect with them on a purified space.

Peppermint is also useful in stimulating dreams and increasing awareness. Use it to work with your angel team on topics of your interest during dream time.

It's also very energizing and helps you thorough your daily activities.

Pine: This essential oil awakens those who are sleeping and enlightens the self to its inner wisdom. Pine can also bring brilliant flashes or insights while connecting ourselves to the angelic realm.

Rose: This essential oil elevates you to the highest vibration of unconditional love. Rose essential oil is a heart opener and helps you to connect with the angelic realm.

Rosemary: This is the remembrance essential oil and helps us to find the answers to our questions. It brings to us information about past lives and also for our life purpose. Rosemary also acts as an energetic protection oil, working with Archangel Michael.

Rosewood: This is an excellent essential oil for meditation; opening the doors to the spiritual realms. It clears the path of communication with the angelic realm.

Sage: This essential oil is one of the strongest oils used for protection and purification. It can be used to purify the environment, to cleanse the aura, and protect ourselves from lower energies. Sage carries the wisdom of the ages and can unveil the secrets of the universe.

Sandalwood: This essential oil helps you to stimulate your awareness elevating your consciousness into the higher realms, allowing yourself to enter into deep state of meditation, visualization, and connection with the spirit realm.

Yarrow: This essential oil helps you to banish negative energies and enhances psychic abilities.

Ylang Ylang: This essential oil tunes our energy with the high vibration of forgiveness, calming our mind and hearts.

How to connect to the angels using essential oils

Here you will find a list of different essential oils to connect with each one of the 15 archangels. You can choose the ones you feel attuned from the lists or let your intuition guide you to incorporate other ones.

You can also elaborate your own essential oil, mixing the oils proposed here on the list or the ones proposed by your intuition.

Once you pick up the essential oils and mix them; you can apply the oil on your skin, and alternately you can diffuse it in your home.

Then start to breathe, relax, listen, and experience the angel (s) you are invoking. Follow your breathing for a couple of minutes and say the prayer proposed by the angel on this chapter. You can also say a prayer from your heart. There is not a strict procedure. My only advice is that you always follow your intuition. The communication happens when the elements are present but most important when you trust in yourself and of course on the angels.

Essential Oils and Archangels

Archangel Ariel

Archangel Ariel is the Patron Saint of Animals, the Environment and the Elements. Ariel is the protector of Mother Earth working closely with planetary concerns. Ariel helps us with manifestation, prosperity, and abundance.

The essential oils you can use to invoke Archangel Ariel are:

Chamomile	Frankincense
Cinnamon	Neroli
Ginger	Sandalwood

Combine the essentials oils with a prayer to help you to manifest abundance and prosperity:

"Archangel Ariel, I call upon your presence now. Please open the door to my financial freedom and allow abundance to flow my way, so I no longer have to worry about money. Help me to become fully capable of making my own living and giving generously to those who need my help."

Archangel Azrael

Archangel Azrael assists souls and helps them in the transition of physical life to the spirit world after death. He also brings healing energy and comfort those on grief. Azrael accompanies us and support us during moments of big transitions in our lives; helping us to see the lessons on these deep transitions.

The essential oils you can use to invoke Archangel Azrael during moments of deep transitions in your life are:

Bergamot	Ginger
Cinnamon	Nutmeg
Clove	Marjoram
Cypress	Rose

Combine the essentials oils with a prayer to help you to bring comfort and peace in your heart, while you go through transitions and physical separation with your beloved ones:

"Archangel Azrael please radiates great compassion and wisdom in my heart, so I can heal pain of unforgiveness, guilt, anger, regret, and find peace in my heart. Please surround my family as we grieve. Heal all emotional pain and comfort us. Remind us we will meet again. Bless those as they leave onto a better place."

Archangel Chamuel

Archangel Chamuel helps you to resolve, heal and strengthen all of your relationships including those with friends, loved ones and others; and also, our careers and work colleagues. He also assists you to connect and heal your inner child. Archangel Chamuel helps us to build strong foundations in our lives and assists us with our life purpose. He is also a great mentor to find inner peace within yourself.

The essential oils you can use to invoke Archangel Chamuel to assist you bringing love, joy and happy in your relationships are:

Benzoin	Jasmine	Orange
Chamomile	Lavender	Rose
Cinnamon	Linden Blossom	Sandalwood
Clove	Mandarin	Vanilla
Coriander	Melissa	Yarrow
Frankincense	Mimosa	Ylang Ylang
Geranium	Neroli	

Combine the essentials oils with a prayer to help you to bring peace and harmony in your relationships and your heart:

"Dear archangel Chamuel, please help me to find inner peace and balance within me so I can find them also around me. Chamuel, please bless me with a positive, happy relationship, love in my life that is lasting, strong, and true."

Archangel Gabriel

Archangel Gabriel assists 'human messengers' and parents. As the patron of communications, Archangel Gabriel is the messenger angel, acting as a 'messenger of God.' Gabriel is the angel who brings man the gifts of mercy and hope; and helps those whose life purpose involves the arts, communication and helps those who deliver spiritual messages. Archangel Gabriel is also the angel of motivation and positive action.

The essential oils you can use to invoke Archangel Gabriel are:

Angelica	Coriander	Myrrh
Anise Star	Dill seed	Narcissus
Basil	Geranium	Neroli
Bay	Lavender	Rose

Benzoin	Lemon Verbena	Rosemary
Cinnamon	Linden Blossom	Spearmint
Clary Sage	Melissa	Wild Orange

Combine the essentials oils with a prayer to help you to live harmoniously, develop your intuition, communicate clearly and listen to the messages of all our senses:

"I humbly invoke the presence of archangel Gabriel in my life. Please help me to have clear and lovely communication with everybody touching my life. Dear Gabriel, please guide me to be patient, so I can listen and understand others. Archangel Gabriel, please use me as an instrument of the heaven realm to deliver messages to others."

Archangel Haniel

Archangel Haniel is the angel of joy and helps us to enjoy harmony, beauty and more grace in our lives. Haniel motivates us to connect immediately with love, peace and gratitude so we can elevate ourselves to high vibrations and communicate with our spiritual helpers. If you've become frustrated and disappointed looking for happiness, call upon Haniel to develop high energetic values to enjoy life and specially your own life.

The essential oils you can use to invoke Archangel Haniel are:

Bay	Lemon	Rose
Carnation	Myrrh	Sandalwood
Chamomile	Neroli	
Grapefruit	Orange	

Combine the essentials oils with a prayer to help you to align your energy with positive emotions of peace, contentment, and gratitude:

"I call upon you, dear archangel Haniel to bring harmony and happiness in my life. Please help me to restore my energy and passion for life. Haniel, please share your grace and wisdom with me, so I can see beauty in all things and assist me to bring harmony in my relationships including the one with myself."

Archangel Jeremiel

Archangel Jeremiel help us to evaluate our lives taking every mistake as a lesson, and any success as a blessing. If you want to re-evaluate your life; if you are under a big change or transition in your life; if you want to solve challenges and problems due to this transition; if you want to learn from this change; if you want to let go past blockages; invoke Archangel Jeremiel. He will help you to find peace and harmony in your life during challenging moments.

The essential oils you can use to invoke Archangel Jeremiel are:

Cinnamon	Lemongrass	Spearmint
Eucalyptus	Peppermint	Sweet Basil
Ginger	Rosemary	Sunflower
Lavender	Roman Chamomile	

Combine the essentials oils with a prayer to help you to go through challenging transitions and find harmony on the process:

"Dear archangel Jeremiel, I call upon you to stand by me. Please help me to be fearless while I learn life lessons. Please help me to review my life surrounding me with your loving light, so I can appreciate the lessons I need to learn. Please help me to release any negative emotion that is holding me back and blocking me to advance in my life. Help me to bring harmony, so I can see the perfection of this Universe and the gifts of the challenging situations."

Archangel Jophiel

Archangel Jophiel is the angel of beauty and art. She helps us to appreciate the beauty around us. Archangel Jophiel helps us to create beauty and bring balance and harmony in our daily lives. Jophiel will help you to shift your perspective from focusing on what is wrong and bad, into seeing the positive, beauty and magic that is all around you. She also brings the energies of illumination and joy.

The essential oils you can use to work with Archangel Jophiel to cleanse your body, mind, and soul are:

Benzoin	Lemon
Bergamot	Narcissus
Chamomile	Neroli

Combine the essentials oils with a prayer to help you to go through challenging transitions and find harmony on the process:

"I invoke the golden yellow light of Archangel Jophiel to help me to manifest beauty within and around me. Please dear Jophiel, help me to clear my thoughts, so they renew my energy cleansing my body, mind and soul. Please help me uplift my vibrations and live in harmony and peace."

The essential oils you can use to work with Archangel Jophiel to balance, restore, and center our inner being are:

Amyris	Lavender	Rosewood
Cedarwood	Lemon	Ylang Ylang
Geranium	Mandarin	
Grapefruit	Orange	

Combine the essentials oils with a prayer to help you to balance and restore your inner being:

"I invoke the golden yellow light of Archangel Jophiel to help me to manifest beauty within and around me. Please dear Jophiel help me to balance the energies of my whole being, and please restore my inner being so I can fully serve others and live a balanced life."

The essential oils you can use to work with Archangel Jophiel to help us with concentration, mental clarity and memory enhancement are:

Basil	Mandarin	Rosemary
Cajeput	Neroli	Spearmint
Cedarwood	Oak Moss	Sweet Fennel
Frankincense	Orange	Tea-tree
Juniper	Palmarosa	

Combine the essentials oils with a prayer to help you with concentration, mental clarity and memory enhancement:

"I invoke the golden yellow light of Archangel Jophiel to help me to manifest beauty within and around me. Please dear Jophiel help me to focus on my heart's intentions. Help me to bring light to my thoughts, so I can have a clear mind to support my soul's mission. Help me to remember the beauty of my inner gifts so I can serve my planet and honor myself."

The essential oils you can use to work with Archangel Jophiel to help you with confidence, self-esteem, and self-expression are:

Basil	Jasmine	Orange

Bergamot	Lemon	Rosemary
Chamomile	Lime	Ylang Ylang
Grapefruit	Mandarin	

Combine the essentials oils with a prayer to invoke Jophiel. This prayer is dedicated to help you to be confident and enhance your self-esteem:

"I invoke the golden yellow light of Archangel Jophiel to help me to bring beauty in my life. Please dear Jophiel help me to appreciate the beauty inside and outside me, so I can shine to the world bringing that inner light wherever I go. Please help me to love and appreciate myself, so I can express the same feeling to every person that arrives in my life."

Archangel Metatron

Metatron is the Archangel to call upon when you need help with divine communion and receiving sacred information through codes and symbols. He aids you to balance your aura and opening your psychic gifts, so you can fulfill your soul mission.

He also helps sensitive children to understand their gifts and teach them how to use those gifts. If you are looking for enlightenment and spiritual growth call upon him.

The essential oils you can use to invoke Archangel Metatron are:

Basil	Geranium	Neroli
Benzoin	Jasmine	Patchouli
Cedarwood	Juniper	Rose
Chamomile	Lavender	Rosemary
Cypress	Lemon	Sandalwood
Frankincense	Mandarin	Ylang Ylang

Combine the essentials oils with a prayer to help you to uplift your energies and connect with your inner gifts:

"I call upon archangel Metatron, to purify my energy and allow me to be a clear and a pure channel of God's love. Dear Metatron, please teach me to use my spiritual gifts and greater powers, so I can be of service to others. Help me to empower myself, recognizing and feeling the potential of my spiritual legacy. Help me to be the light and make a difference in this world."

Archangel Michael

Archangel Michael assists you with releasing lower energies of fear or worry and also can provide you guidance to fulfill your life purpose. He is the angel of protection and gives you courage to overcome any obstacle in your path. Michael also brings us energy, vitality, motivation, and motivates us to be confident.

The essential oils you can use to work with Archangel Michael for protection, safety, and empowerment are:

Anise Star	Geranium	Oak moss
Aniseed	Ginger	Pine
Black Pepper	Hyssop	Rosemary
Cajeput	Juniper	Sage
Carnation	Lavender	Sweet Fennel
Clary Sage	Lime	Tea-tree
Clove	Melissa	Thyme
Cumin	Mimosa	Valerian
Frankincense	Myrrh	Yarrow

Combine the essentials oils with a prayer to help you to feel protected and secured:

"Archangel Michael, please come and connect with me at this present moment. I ask you for the great protection of the heaven aligning myself with my highest and the greatest good. Surround me with your wings of strength, courage and protection, so I feel I am not alone, and I am fully protected by you and the angels of protection."

The essential oils you can use to work with Archangel Michael for banishing negativity, calming anxiety, and dispelling fears and phobias are:

Bergamot	Lavender	Rose
Camphor	Lime	Sage
Chamomile	Mandarin	Sandalwood
Eucalyptus	Neroli Sweet	Marjoram
Hyssop	Peppermint	Ylang Ylang

Combine the essentials oils with a prayer to help you to banish negativity and dispel fears and phobias:

"Archangel Michael, I ask that you use your sword of light to cut away all doubt, fear, guilty or negativity which is around me. Cut any and all cords which are draining my energy across the lines of time and assist me in reintegrating my light and personal power back into my being now."

Use Wild Orange to help you to energize and uplift the mind and body. Connect with Archangel Michael to vitalize your body, mind and spirit."

Archangel Raguel

Archangel Raguel assists with healing relationships as he is the perfect mediator and can help bringing harmony and co-operation into any situation. Call upon him to understand the nature of misunderstandings. Understanding where they come from and how to avoid them will strengthen relationships and prevent disagreements.

The essential oils you can use to invoke Archangel Raguel are:

Patchouli
Orange
Ylang Ylang

Combine the essentials oils with a prayer to help you restore peace and serenity in your relationships:

"Dear Archangel Raguel, thank you for bringing peace, harmony and to restore all of my relationships. Thank you for helping me to be a good friend to myself and all others."

Archangel Raphael

Archangel Raphael is the doctor of the heaven and also the 'patron of travelers.' He overseas any journey in your life: physical and spiritual. Archangel Raphael guides healers to choose the best treatment for people coming for healing.

The essential oils you can use to work with Archangel Raphael for regeneration, renewal and healing are:

Carnation	Lavender	Pine
Cedarwood	Lemon	Rose
Chamomile	Neroli	Sandalwood
Clove	Myrrh	Spearmint
Juniper	Palmarosa	Thyme

Combine the essentials oils with a prayer to help you to bring healing, renewal, and regeneration:

"Dear archangel Raphael, please heal my physical body of all pain, illness, and suffering. I ask for vibrant health. Please wrap my body in your emerald green light until there is no ill. Please reveal my perfectly healed body. Let me be whole. Raphael, please help me to accept I am already divinely healed."

Archangel Raziel

Archangel Raziel helps with the understanding of esoteric knowledge and higher wisdom. He brings magic to our lives, motivating us to remember our unique inner gifts; and helps us to open up to higher levels of psychic abilities.

The essential oils you can use to work with Archangel Raziel to open your third eye are:

Bay	Lemon Verbena	Rose
Benzoin	Lime	Rosewood
Carrot seed	Myrrh	Sage
Cinnamon	Narcissus	Sandalwood
Jasmine	Neroli	

The essential oils you can use to work with Archangel Raziel to access higher guidance, using divine abilities, and enhancing spiritual awareness are:

Angelica	Clove Bud	Narcissus
Bay	Frankincense	Peppermint
Benzoin	Lemon Verbena	Rosewood
Carrot seed	Linden Blossom	Sage
Cinnamon	Myrrh	Sandalwood
Clary Sage	Mimosa	

Combine the essentials oils with a prayer to help you to enhance your psychic abilities and spiritual awareness:

"Dear archangel Raziel, you know the gifts and wisdom of the universe. Today I ask you to show me these spiritual secrets that I am ready to know. Please, empower me to apply what I have learned, so I can live with wisdom and spiritual insight fulfilling my soul's mission on Earth."

Archangel Sandalphon

Archangel Sandalphon is the protector of all nature caring for Earth planet, presents people's prayers to God, and directs the music in heaven. He guides the prayers to heaven, so they may be heard by the Creator.

The essential oils you can use to invoke Archangel Sandalphon are:

Myrrh	Petitgrain
Patchouli	Ravensara
Petigrain	Sandalwood
Pine	Yarrow

Combine the essentials oils with a prayer to ask for answers to our prayers:

"I call upon you, archangel Sandalphon to stand by me. Please guide my prayers to heaven so that they may be heard. Please allow me to hear the songs you sing, and the messages you carry for me. Please bring the answers and loving guidance back to me, so I can easily hear them."

Archangel Uriel

Archangel Uriel bring the light of God illuminating any situation. He also gives prophetic warnings, intellectual information, creative insights and practical solution. Uriel works closely to mother nature, especially regarding elements of weather.

The essential oils you can use to invoke Archangel Uriel are:

Basil	Grapefruit	Sandalwood
Black Pepper	Lavender	Sweet Fennel
Carnation	Mandarin	Sweet Marjoram
Chamomile	Melissa	Thyme
Clove	Neroli	Yarrow
Frankincense	Pettigrain	
Ginger	Rose	

Combine the essentials oils with a prayer to ask for illumination on any challenging situations:

"Dear archangel Uriel, I call upon you to stand by me. Please release all emotional fears and blocks. Please help me soothe all conflict in my life and replace it with peace, clarity, insight. I ask you, fill me with the knowingness of who I really am. Please surround me with your divine light. Please fill me with love, serenity, and confidence."

Archangel Zadkiel

Archangel Zadkiel is the archangel of 'mercy' and 'benevolence' assisting us in letting go of judgement and unforgiveness and helping us with compassion and mercy towards others and ourselves. Zadkiel motivates us to bring joy, love, forgiveness, and freedom in our lives. This archangel assists memory retention and functions and study. He is also the archangel of the Violet Flame and transmutation.

The essential oils you can use to call upon Archangel Zadkiel to open the Crown chakra invoking divine spiritual wisdom, forgiveness, understanding, compassion are:

Anise Star	Cypress	Pine
Basil	Frankincense	Rosemary
Benzoin	Hyssop	Rosewood
Cedarwood	Lavender	Sage
Chamomile	Lemon	Sandalwood
Clary Sage	Myrrh	Verben

Combine the essentials oils with a prayer to ask for divine connection invoking archangel Zadkiel:

"Dear archangel Zadkiel, I call on you now to stand by me. Please shine your energy of forgiveness, compassion and spiritual understanding, so I could be able to find a way to forgive those who have hurt me in the past. Please help me to move forward with a greater peace of mind and find freedom for my soul. I trust every detail is taken care of with divine grace, harmony and wisdom."

The essential oils you can use to call upon Archangel Zadkiel to purify your aura, clear your space, transmute negative energies into positives, and to invoke the Violet Flame are:

Basil	Hyssop	Pine
Bay	Juniper	Rosemary
Camphor	Lavender	Rose

Cedarwood	Lemon	Sage
Citronella	Lemon Grass	Sandalwood
Clary Sage	Melissa	Spearmint
Cypress	Myrrh	Thyme
Eucalyptus	Neroli	Valerian
Frankincense	Peppermint	Verbena

Combine the essentials oils with a prayer to ask for transmutation of energies invoking the Violet flame:

"Dear Archangel Zadkiel, I call upon you to invoke the sacred presence of the Violet Flame into my life now. I ask you for transmutation of any low energy that is holding me back from the freedom of my soul. Please transmute any shadow into the purity of the Cosmic Light. Please help me to understand that I AM divine freedom in manifestation, that I AM filled with happiness, forgiveness, joy, and mercy. Thank you for your divine help!"

CHAPTER6: ANGELS AND CRYSTALS

Crystals have been revered since the dawn of civilization as having sacred and healing powers. Crystals embody in the physical and higher qualities of Divine light and Spirit. Crystals have a strong affinity with the angelic realms, and a few beautiful crystals arranged on your altar will attract angelic presences. The crystals' vibrations enable us to attune and to communicate with angels, archangels, to receive their wisdom, guidance, and healing.

In the following lines, you will find information about choosing, cleaning, and activating your crystals. The second part of this chapter is dedicated to the particular relationship between the archangels and the crystals working with their energy.

Choosing a crystal

I believe the crystals choose us to be their guardian. Choosing a crystal becomes an agreement of both parts. When you choose a crystal follow your intuition, open your heart to communicate with the spirit of the elemental. You can also follow your intuition or scan the crystal.

You will feel energies while you are choosing. The sensations you could experience while choosing a crystal are:

- Heat emanating from the crystal
- Cold energy
- Pulsing or vibrating
- A sensation of balance and wholeness

- Tingling in your hands
- A flow of energy that may even feel like an electric charge

Just follow your intuition and be ready to work as a team with them!

Cleansing a crystal

It's essential to cleanse a crystal before you use it; to remove any negative vibrations that it may absorbed form anyone who has previously handle it. Here are few simple methods to cleanse:

- Water method: Hold your crystal under cleared running water
- Earth method: Bury your crystal in the ground and leave it for at least 24 hours
- Fire method: Surround your crystals with tea candles for few hours until they complete to burned out
- Smudge method: Smudge your crystal allowing the element of the air to transmute any negative vibration
- Flower method: Gather few flowers or petals and place them in a clear-glass container. Bury the crystal under the petals and let it there for 24 hours

Activating your crystals with the help of your angels

Once the crystals have been cleansed, they may be activated or intentioned with your Angels. Simply place the crystal on your altar, light a candle, burn essential oils, and relax. Invite your angels to come to your sacred space and take the crystal close to your heart.

You can say a prayer like the one above to activate your crystals:

"I activate and intention these crystals to the angelic realms as a bridge between heaven and earth; to deepen my connection and heighten my receptivity to the guidance of the angelic streams of consciousness."

Crystals for connecting with the Archangels

ARIEL

Keywords
Environmental issues, animal welfare and healing, healing plants, healing the planet.

Crystals
Aventurine: Strong healing energy for body, mind and spirit. Balance erratic emotions.

Emerald: Stone of loyalty and successful love. Open and activate the heart chakra. Bring harmony to all areas of your life.

Moonstone: Harmonize one's feeling with their higher self, bring feelings into awareness.

Rose Quartz: Love stone. It helps to open the heart for true love and friendship. Nurturing, comforting energy, brings inner peace, and teach us to love ourselves.

AZRAEL

Keywords
Peaceful passing over, comfort to the grieving and heartbroken, development of counseling skills.

Crystals

Ametrine: A fusion of citrine and amethyst. Manifestation of one's visions. Bring our deeper dreams to reality.

Fluorite: Enhance memory, intellect, and concentration. Bring wisdom.

Smokey quartz: Activate survival instincts. Ground light force into the physical body. Focus. Good for fatigue. Enhance sexuality and fertility.

Yellow Calcite: It is a clearer of accumulated self-doubt, giving you the opportunity for a clean emotional state.

CHAMUEL

Keywords
Finding new love, friendship, career, job, lost objects, peace in relationships, healing soul mate relationships.

Crystals

Aventurine: Strong healing energy for body, mind and spirit. Balance erratic emotions.

Fluorite: Enhance memory, intellect, and concentration. Bring wisdom.

Jade: It inspires and induces ambition toward the accomplishment of objectives.

Rose Quartz: Love stone. It helps to open the heart for true love and friendship. Nurturing, comforting energy, bring inner peace and teach us to love ourselves.

GABRIEL

Keywords
Conception, pregnancy and birth, adoption, early childhood issues, life path of spiritual teachers and writers.

Crystals

Angelite: Symbol of communication of love and light to the world. Helper in spiritual journeys and dispels anger.

Aquamarine: Encourage the expression of one's truth. Reduce fears and mental tension.

Celestite: Dream recall, expands consciousness, facilitate astral traveling.

Moonstone: Harmonize one's feeling with their higher self, bring feelings into awareness.

HANIEL

Keywords
Menstrual cycle, hormonal issues, fertility, personal harmony, balance, honoring sensitivity.

Crystals

Angelite: Symbol of communication of love and light to the world. Helper in spiritual journeys and dispel anger.

Howlite: Facilitate awareness, encourage emotional expression and assist in the elimination of pain, stress and/or rage.

Moonstone: Harmonize one's feeling with their higher self, brings feelings into awareness.

Selenite: Stimulate brain activity, expand awareness, develop telepathy, symbolize the clearest state of mind attainable.

JEREMIEL

Keywords
Healing unhealed patterns, conducting life reviews, emotional healing.

Crystals

Amethyst: Awakener of the third eye. Develop intuition and awareness. Facilitate meditation, calming and tranquility.

Fluorite: Enhance memory, intellect, and concentration. Bring wisdom.

Garnet: Stone of health. Stimulate kundalini. Raise one's internal fire, bringing the creative powers to manifest.

Rhodochrosite: Relieve and calm down the heart, enhance the creative process, peace and warmth.

JOPHIEL

Keywords
Clearing negative energies, artistic projects, development of inner beauty, radiating grace.

Crystals

Citrine: Stone of success, money, abundance, prosperity. Raise self-esteem. Good luck for business projects.

Golden Labradorite: It is a stone that assists you on your self-empowerment. It has the masculine energy of the sun, so it is a stone to use to balance energy with feminine energy.

Moonstone: Harmonize one's feeling with their higher self, bring feelings into awareness.

Rose Quartz: Love stone. It helps to open the heart for true love and friendship. Nurturing, comforting energy, brings inner peace and teach us to love ourselves.

METATRON

Keywords
Chakra clearing, issues with children, raising spiritual awareness.

Crystals

Labradorite: For self-discovery, it is excellent for awakening one's own awareness of inner spirit, intuition and psychic abilities.

Kyanite: This crystal is used for opening the mind centers, enhancing telepathic and psychic abilities, bridging gaps in all communication efforts, and providing a link for transmitting or receiving healing energy.

Topaz: Topaz is a symbol of love and affection; and has been said to be an aid to one's sweetness and disposition.

Watermelon tourmaline: It soothes the heart and relieves anger or resentment. Used in meditation. It assists with calming mind and emotions, allowing us to release stress.

MICHAEL

Keywords
Protection, safety, overcoming fears, life purpose, cutting energetic cords, fixing any mechanical item including computers, build self-esteem and self-worth.

Crystals

Angelite: Symbol of communication of love and light to the world. Helper in spiritual journeys and dispel anger.

Lapis Lazuli: Open third eye attaining wisdom. Associated with virtues of courage, insight, strength, clarity, and compassion.

Sodalite: Awakener of the third eye which prepares the mind to receive the inner sight and intuitive knowledge.

Sugilite: Wear or carry Sugilite to create a warm, protective 'shield of Light,' keeping the wearer impervious to negativity and the disharmony of others.

RAGUEL

Keywords
Conflict resolution, justice and fairness, harmony.

Crystals

Aquamarine: Encourage the expression of one's truth. Very helpful to overcome fears and ease your mind.

Blue Lace Agate: It is a stone of communication, helping those who have difficulty being heard by others, or who need confidence and articulation to share their truths.

Kyanite: This crystal is used for opening the mind centers, enhancing telepathic and psychic abilities, bridging gaps in all communication efforts, and providing a link for transmitting or receiving healing energy.

Sodalite: Awakener of the third eye which prepares the mind to receive the inner sight and intuitive knowledge.

RAPHAEL

Keywords
Physical healing, good health, assistance to healers, travel safety.

Crystals

Aventurine: Wonderful for inner and outward journeys. Balance healing for body, mind and spirit.

Chrysoprase: Known for manifesting optimism, joy, and happiness. Chrysoprase is one of the best antidepressants in the world of crystal healing.

Emerald: Stone of loyalty and successful love. Open and activate the heart chakra. Bring harmony into all areas of your life.

Malachite: Stone of balance, abundance, manifestation and intention. Malachite absorbs energy and draws emotions to the surface. It clears and activates all Chakras.

RAZIEL

Keywords
Clairvoyance, manifestation, third eye healing, esoteric learning, past life healing.

Crystals

Amethyst: Awakener of the third eye and crown chakra. Develop awareness and incite to be intuitive. Facilitates meditation, calming and tranquility.

Diamond: Represent faithfulness, love, purity, innocence, and relationships filled with love. It inspires creativity, ingenuity, faith, endurance, and help in manifesting abundance in all areas of life. Diamond is a symbol of the richness of the Self.

Labradorite: Protect one's aura. Keep the aura cleared, balanced, free from energy leaks. Bring the light of other planetary beings to the soul of the person using the stone.

Smokey quartz: Activate survival instincts. Ground light force into the physical body. Focusing. Good for fatigue. Enhance sexuality and fertility.

SANDALPHON

Keywords
Healing through music and nature.

Crystals

Amazonite: It has healing powers to help with physical ailments, emotional issues. Very useful for in Energy Healing and Chakra Balancing. It helps with stress, healing traumas, and soothing energies in the home and workplace.

Apatite: Apatite stones encourage creativity, increase inner strength, and clear mental blocks.

Aquamarine: Encourage the expression of one's truth. Reduce fears and mental tension.

Turquoise: It is a stone of protection, strong and opaque, yet soothing to the touch, healing to the eye, as if carved from an azure heaven and slipped to earth.

URIEL

Keywords
Uncovering divine wisdom, intellectual learning and growth.

Crystals

Amber: Give courage and confidence to make any changes needed in life. Revitalizer and mood stabilizer.

Hematite: Stone of protection and grounding. Seals one's auric field against negativities.

Obsidian: Spiritual protector. Helps one to understand and face their deepest fears.

Rubi: Stimulate life force energies. Enhance passion, courage, optimism and determination.

ZADKIEL

Keywords
Memory, spiritual teaching and learning, healing the heart.

Crystals

Amethyst: Awakener of the third eye. Develop intuition and awareness. Facilitate meditation, calming and tranquility.

Ametrine: Fusion of citrine and amethyst. Manifestation of one's visions. Bring our deeper dreams to reality.

Fluorite: Enhance memory, intellect, and concentration. Bring wisdom.

Jade: It inspire and induce ambition toward the accomplishment of objectives.

CHAPTER 7: ARCHANGELS AND CHAKRAS

Before this chapter is introduced, I would like to clarify, there are many perspectives to the topic of archangels and chakras. For example, some people associate an archangel with a chakra that is probably not mention on this chapter, and that is also fine. Everyone has a connection, and this connection is interpreted based on their own experiences. I reiterate, if something mentioned here does not resonate with your experience, please do not take it. Follow your intuition. It is your best advisor.

The material presented in this book is based in 18 years of my personal work experience with angels, spirits of the Earth and Cosmos, as well as my relationship with the Ascended Masters and the wisdom of the Seven Rays.

How to balance your chakras with the angels

Angels have a definite affinity to Chakra Healing, call upon them for assistance on clearing, balancing, and healing your chakras. Your life energy depends on the flow of these vortexes of energy called chakras. To maintain and regulate their flow, this chapter contains information and self-care about each one of them, as well as angel work and mantras that will help maintain these vortices cleared and in balance.

Energies can be combined by working with the Archangel of the chakra, crystals, herbs, essential oils and practices recommended. Follow your intuition and choose what resonates within you.

At the end of this book, guided exercises to work on clearing and balancing your chakras are proposed to enhance the work with your angels.

What is chakra?

Chakra comes from the sanskrit meaning 'wheel or disk.' These energy centers are located along our spine and associated to all processes, glands and organs in our bodies.

You are energy. All living things are created by and composed of energy. When these wheels or energy centers are functioning correctly, you can experience a balance between your body, mind and spirit.

There are seven main chakras, which align the spine, starting from the base of the spine through to the crown of the head.
Each chakra has its own vibrational energy, color, and rules some functions of our human body. This book will cover the main 7 chakras.

On the angelic realm, every energetic vortex is overseen by an archangel that works balancing and healing the energy center, and the organs associated to the specific chakra.

To enhance the practice of balancing the chakras, use essential oils and crystals associated with the archangel regulating the chakra. A fantastic and complete healing experience mixing the information proposed for archangels, essential oils, and crystals is useful when you perform 'Energy Healing.'

The appendix section of this book provides exercises you can do at your own pace for chakra balancing and chakra clearing.

1.   Root Chakra - I am

The root chakra is the first chakra, and its vitality is related to the Earth element. This chakra is found at the base of the spine. This is the base and the structure on which we build our life, and it's related to safety and grounding. This energetic vortex helps us to anchor our energy into the dimension of manifestation.

Essential concerns related to the root chakra are instinct, security, rooting, survival, grounding, family, belonging to a tribe, limits, and new beginnings.

Body parts related to the root chakra are coccyx, anus, large intestine, adrenal glands, lower back, legs, feet and bones. Reproductive glands controlling sexual development and secrete sex hormones.

Principal enemy: tribal or family beliefs, fears, don't feel safe, don't trust to get jobs or money needing.

Color: red

Essential characteristics of the root chakra are:

- Safeness
- Preservation, survival
- Basic needs and sustentation
- Grounding and rooting
- Structure and base of life
- Support
- Sense of belonging to a tribe

Signs of an imbalanced root chakra

- Exaggerated negativity
- Disproportioned feeling of insecurity
- Over sense of materialism, imbalance between physical concerns and spiritual concerns
- Pessimism and sarcasm
- Eating disorders
- Selfishness and avarice

Here are some *questions to ask yourself*. Answer them honestly to check blockage in your first chakra:

1. In what areas of your life do you not feel safe?
2. In what areas of your life do you feel there is not enough?
3. In what areas of your life do you feel you have no control or choice?
4. Are you procrastinating or not having discipline to achieve your goals?
5. Do you trust life? Do you feel supported by the Universe?
6. Do you trust yourself to make good decisions for a happy and balanced life?
7. Are you able to easily make decisions?
8. Are you able to materialize your dreams or goals?
8. Pain? Stiffness? Sciatica? Constipation?
9. How do you feel your hips, pelvis, knees and ankles?
10. What about abundance, how do you feel about it?

How to balance the root chakra

- Walk barefoot in nature
- Understand your body's messages (feel your emotions and let them go)
- Eat healthy
- Rest and sleep
- Dance (archaic music of any primitive people)
- Red color visualization
- Massage and pedicure
- Trust in the Universe
- Develop tolerance, respect and compassion towards others

Herbs and foods for root chakra

- Dandelion root tea is a good supplement for treating depression, gallbladder or high blood pressure
- Try to consume foods with roots like: carrots, potatoes, yucca, yams, turmeric, sweet potatoes, rutabagas, or anything on red tones as tomatoes, beet, red peppers, radicchio and red onions

Essential oils for root chakra

Benzoin, Cedar, Clove, Patchouli, Vetivert

Crystals for root chakra

Agate, black Tourmaline, Bloodstone, Garnet, Hematite, Obsidian, red Calcite, red Coral, red Jasper, Ruby, Smoky Quartz

Working with ascended masters

Artemis, Ashtar, Athena, Brigit, Kali, Lugh, Tara

Uriel, the archangel of the root chakra

Archangel Uriel is one of four main archangels of the four directions mentioned in many ancestral texts. The other archangels are Michael, Gabriel and Raphael. Uriel is one of the seven archangels known as 'Angels of the Rays.' He is known as the keeper of the Ruby Ray of Light working for humanity for the root chakra. He is the angel of the North direction associated with the Earth element and regulating the energy of this vortex. Uriel is known for bringing grounding, security, balance. Guides and supports light workers in their mission on the planet. He boosts with an entrepreneur energy those who want to start a new business. Uriel helps ground us to this planet and everything related to it. Call upon Uriel when you feel insecure and unprotected; and when you need to root yourself to your home on Planet Earth.

Use the following prayer to work with archangel Uriel to balance your root chakra:

"The Presence of Uriel and his stability ground me. His energy from mother Earth roots me. The energy of the planet womb makes me feel at peace consciousness, connection with my ancestors, and freedom guide my path."

Affirmation: use as a mantra to balance your root chakra

"I release fear, knowing that I am totally loved, supported, guided and protected by my celestial helpers. I am a child of the Universe, and I am in peace, free, protected and secure."

2. Sacral Chakra - I feel

The sacral chakra is the second chakra, and its energy is associated to Water element. This chakra works directly with our emotions and thoughts.

The sacral chakra is found in the abdomen area, just below the belly. This is your point of change, the polarity, the duality. It is associated with the emotional body, the center of feelings and sensations; influenced by the center of pleasure where sensuality and sexual desires are expressed. When this chakra is open, you allow yourself to 'feel' the world. It supports the formation of our identity and how we relate with others.

Essential concerns related with the sacral chakra are emotions, sexuality, transformation, creativity, sensuality, pleasure, relationships and feminine divine.

Body parts related to the sacral chakra are bladder, kidneys, prostate, testes, ovaries, hips. On this energy center, the immune system and metabolism are regulated by the adrenal glands.

Principal enemy: guilt

Color: orange

Essential characteristics of the sacral chakra are:

- Emotions and feelings
- Relationships (love, family, friends, colleagues)
- Sexuality, sensuality, pleasure
- Creativity
- Inspiration
- Fantasies

Signs of an imbalanced sacral chakra

- Dependency, codependency with any person or behavior
- Addiction (any kind including toxic relationships)
- Allowing emotions to control your actions
- Been apathetic and allowing the mind to guide your actions
- Sexual obsessions
- Fantasizing most of the time
- Lack of sexual desire or satisfaction
- Constant mood swings

Here are some *questions to ask yourself.* Answer them honestly to check blockage in your second chakra:

1. What attracts you?
2. How attractive do you feel? Do you feel beautiful/handsome?
3. Are you confident about your self-image?
4. Did you have any incidents in your childhood where you felt ugly?
5. Do you feel your emotions governs your life? Or do you use emotional intelligence while you relate to others?
6. Are you often driven by pleasure? Or do you have a balance between pleasure and responsibilities?
7. Can you balance passion and discipline? Are you able to find a neutral point to satisfy both parts?
8. Are you living your passion?
9. Do you express passion for life?
10. Are you happy with your relationships?

How to balance the sacral chakra

- Be thankful for your body
- Be thankful for your gender (woman or man)

- Be happy and thankful to be part of the Universe
- Feel that we deserve to be happy and have abundance in our lives
- Move your hips and belly
- Pelvis rotation
- Hot bath
- Swimming
- Hula hopping
- Massage and sexual activity

Herbs and foods for the sacral chakra

- Apricot fruit gives you clarity in your mind and flexibility in your body
- Calendula petals boost your creative and self-confidence
- Damiana is an aphrodisiac to enhance your sexual activities
- Orange brings stamina and increases your mental activity
- Jasmine flower makes you feel happy and motivated in life
- Coriander stimulates confidence, self-esteem and optimism
- Orange color food such as carrots, melon, apricots, cantaloupe, mangoes, nectarines, peaches, papaya, oranges, grapefruit, passion fruit, sweet potatoes, pumpkin, orange peppers, sweetcorn

Essential oils for sacral chakra

Carrot Seed, Dill, Geranium, Hyssop, Jasmine, Marjoram, Neroli, Orange, Rose, Sandalwood, Tangerine, Texas Cedarwood

Crystals for sacral chakra

Amber, red and brown Aventurine, Carnelian, Citrine, golden Labradorite, Moonstone, orange Calcite, red Garnet, red Jasper, Topaz

Working with ascended masters

Devi, Ishtar, Krishna and Oonagh

Chamuel, the archangel of the sacral chakra

Chamuel is the archangel of pure love. He helps you to switch from moments of sadness to inspiring moments by infusing love to your heart. Chamuel helps create, reestablish, revive, and promote relationships as well as encounter your soul mate. Chamuel also helps establish solid and long-lasting bases on any kind of relationships.

Chamuel helps with world peace, career, life purpose, creativity, artistic path, and finding lost items. He is an excellent counselor for addictions and to overcome substance abuse.

You can use the following prayer to work with archangel Chamuel in order to balance your sacral chakra:

"I am love, I am a divine light. I know my angels want I see that with clarity. I call upon archangel Chamuel, so he can help me see what I cannot see. I call forth archangel Chamuel to assist me to activate my second chakra, so I can be able to create harmonious relationships in my life. Chamuel guides me to attract healthy, long-lasting and meaningful relationship that help me evolve as it is already established on my soul's map.
Please be me counselor so I can act with unconditional love respecting the path of everyone that touch my life. That all my be part of the divine plan, so I can be part of the divine plan of peace in the whole planet and in the whole Universe. And so it is."

Affirmation to use as mantra to balance your sacral chakra

"I feel and express my emotions safely, so I can bring harmony into my relationships. I express creativity and inspiration all around me, and people receive it with gratitude and love. I am blissful, joyful, attractive, beautiful as I am, and I live a passionate life."

3. Solar Plexus - I do

The solar plexus chakra is the third chakra. Its energy is based on the Fire element. This chakra is found in the solar plexus area, at the beginning of your stomach, just below your ribs. This is your point of power, autonomy, will, energy, personal power, mental ability, transformation, metabolism and personality.

The solar plexus chakra purifies the lower chakras to continue ascending to the heart chakra. Here you become the creator of your life. You also find your role in society. This is the place where your inner sun radiates its power and energy. The sun has been important in all ancestral cultures: Ra (Egyptians), Inti (Incas), Tonatiuih (Aztecs), Ku-Kuul-Kaan (Mayas), Vishnu/Indra (Hindu). This is the place where your inner sun shines to the world!

Essential concerns: solar plexus chakra is related to your personal power, intelectual skills, ability to decide and choose, create ideas, innovate your reality, expression of your inner personality.

Body parts: solar plexus chakra is related to the pancreas, liver, gallbladder, spleen. This energy center is supervised by the pancreas, regulating the metabolism.

Principal enemy: shame

Color: yellow

Essential characteristics of the solar plexus chakra are:

- Inner power
- Will and ability to decide and choose
- Taking responsibility for acts and choices
- Mental abilities
- Intellect competences
- Point of view and personal judgement
- Personality, integrity
- Confidence, self-esteem
- Discipline
- Autonomy, self-determination, independence

Signs of an imbalanced solar plexus chakra

- Exaggerated authority
- Control others and situations
- Being controlled by others
- Being obsessed with details
- Being manipulative
- Abuse of power against others
- Lack of purpose
- Lack of ambition
- Lost in your path, do not follow any direction
- Having many plans but lacking energy to focus on materializing them

Here are some *questions to ask yourself*. Answer them honestly to check blockage in your third chakra:

1. Do you feel constantly fatigued and lazy?
2. Do you have eating problems? Are you overeating?
3. Do you manipulate others? Do you think only in what you want not considering others?
4. Do you feel others manipulate you, and you follow them?
5. Do you bully others or try to dominate them?
6. Do you feel insecure about leading others?
7. Do you lack self-confidence in any area of your life?
8. Are you trying to get the approval of others, even your parents?
9. Do you have addictive tendencies?
10. Do you have low self-esteem?
11. Do you let others to invade your boundaries?
12. Do you suffer from a digestive problems or issues?
13. Do you suffer from stomach upset or gas issues?
14. Are you co-dependent in a relationship?

How to balance the solar plexus chakra

- Accept mistakes. We are all human beings. We are learning
- Trust in yourself. Your soul already knows what is good for you
- Express your desire to change. Change will create action in your life
- Action = Act, move, create, so today embrace the role of the creator of your life
- Don't let the criticism of others bother you or block you
- Release and let it go. Nothing stays in your life forever. Be brave, give to the Universe what no longer serves you
- Take a sunbath
- Laugh at yourself. Be flexible with the image you have about yourself

Herbs and foods for solar plexus chakra

- Eat a plant-based diet with carbohydrates such as pasta, rice, tortillas, noodles
- Drink herbal teas, such as chamomile, lemon, lime, lemon balm, lemongrass, lemonade
- Eat yellow food such as banana, apricots, butternut squash, nectarines, yellow potatoes, yellow tomatoes, yellow beets, yellow peppers

Essential oils for solar plexus chakra

Balsam, Benzoin, Bergamot, Chamomile, Clary Sage, Cypress, Dill,

Elemi, Fennel, Frankincense, Geranium, Hyssop, Juniper, Lavender, Lemon, Marjoram, Myrrh, Needle, Neroli, Peppermint, Rosemary, Sage

Crystals for solar plexus chakra

Amber, Citrine, golden Calcite, golden Sunstone, Tiger's Eye, Topaz, yellow Calcite, yellow Tourmaline, yellow Jasper

Working with ascended masters

Pele, Sanat Kumara

Jophiel, the archangel of the solar plexus chakra

Archangel Jophiel name literally means 'beauty of God.' Jophiel is said to have guarded the Tree of Life and was the angel who escorted Adam and Eve from the Garden of Eden with her flaming sword. This sword helps to cut any illusion, pain in our heart and confusion in the mind. We call upon Jophiel when we want to make good decisions that are aligned to our soul path and life purpose. Being the angel of illumination, Jophiel can be called when we need to focus on studying, or when we want to pass victorious a test or exam.

You can call her also, when you are experiencing depression, disappointment or rejection in your life. She will help you see with beauty the lessons of this chapter, bringing you motivation and hope to overcome it. Jophiel always remind us that life is beautiful and a gift of God.

You can use the following prayer to work with archangel Jophiel in order to balance your solar plexus chakra:

" Archangel Jophiel, please help me to see the beauty in this situation that I am not able to understand. Please fulfill my life with optimism, joy, hope, and goodness, so I will be able to overcome this lesson with all the love that I deserve, and everyone deserves. Help me to cover any sadness or painful moment of my life with the magnificence love of the creation. Let me understand that everything is following a divine plan and all it's well."

Affirmation to use as mantra to balance your solar plexus chakra

"I am always successful and powerful in all the adventures of my soul. I am a powerful creator of my life."

4. Heart Chakra - I love

The heart chakra is the fourth chakra, and its energy is based on Air element. The heart chakra is found at the center of the chest, between the breasts. This is your point of love, breathing, balance, union, healing, inner child and compassion.

This is the point of extreme healing because here we discover that only infinite love heals. The fourth chakra act as a divine bridge connecting the lower and upper chakras unifying your earthly and spiritual hopes.

At this point, we experience giving love and receiving love balancing these energies.

Forgiveness is a special key to get healed; and when this chakra is balanced, we can really work tapping into the power of unconditional love.

The essential concerns related with the heart chakra are: the ability to love, connection between earthly and divine hopes, surpass and go beyond the limitations of the ego, understanding and practice unconditional love and divine connection with everything.

The body parts related with the heart chakra are lungs, heart, circulatory system, arms, hands, blood, skin and upper back. On this energetic center, the thymus gland is in charge of regulating the immune system.

Principal enemy: heart pain, heart suffering and victimization

Color. Green. The second color for this chakra is pink or the tone of the rose quartz crystal

Essential characteristics of the heart chakra are:

- Love for everyone including inner love
- Relationships including the one with myself
- Compassion and forgiveness
- Believe in your path and everyone's path
- Transformation
- Be able to feel the sorrow and grief for someone we loved, and be able to release it

Signs of an imbalanced heart chakra

- Not accepting other's people point of view and being defensive
- Competitive and jealous of others
- Having respiratory and circulatory issues

- Having heart disease conditions
- Being codependent or make feel another person codependent of yourself
- Playing the role of the hero most of the time or the victim
- Not being able to feel compassion for others
- Not respecting other's path
- Not being able to forgive
- Feeling depressed and segregated

Here are some *questions to ask yourself*. Answer them honestly to check if you are blocked in your fourth chakra:

1. Do you give and receive love without difficulty?
2. Are you able to forgive others to liberate your spirit? Even if it was not your fault?
3. Are you able to feel compassion towards others, including animals?
4. Do you have circulatory problems?
5. Do you have issues in your heart or lungs?
6. Are you able to express your emotions?
7. How do you manage stress?
8. Do you feel your heart beating fast when you are in a stressful situation?
9. Are you responsible for your acts?
10. Or do you feel guilty even for things you didn't do?

How to balance the heart chakra

- Give and receive love
- Be in contact with flowers and smell their fragrance
- Charity work
- Practice forgiveness (to yourself and others)
- Practice reiki
- Take a walk in nature
- Give with no expectation
- Inner Child Therapy
- Breathing exercises
- Practice self-love and self-compassion to your body, to your thoughts, and your feelings
- Engage in activities that feed your heart
- Express your gratitude

Herbs and foods for heart chakra

- Try the following herbal teas: green tea, hawthorn berry, hibiscus, tulsi (holy basil), ginger, lemongrass, linden
- Eat a diet low in fat, high in omega 3's: salmon, cod liver oil, oysters sardines, anchovies, flax seeds, chia seeds, walnuts; and dark leafy vegetables, like kale and spinach, swiss chard, sprouts, collards, brussels sprouts
- Eat allium family onions, leeks, and especially garlic
- Eat green food as: celery, avocados, green peppers, spinach, zucchini, broad beans, bok choy, cabbage, broccoli, green apples, pears, and kiwi
- Take green supplements as: spirulina, chlorella, barley grass, and wheatgrass

Essential oils for heart chakra

Benzoin, Bergamot, Cinnamon, Cove, Elemi, Eucalyptus, Geranium, Jasmine, Lavender, Lime, Linden Blossom, Mandarin, Mint, Neroli, Peppermint, Rose, Rosemary, Sandalwood, Tea Tree

Crystals for heart chakra

Aventurine, Chrysoprase, Emerald, Jade, Malachite, Peridote, pink Calcite, pink Kunzite, pink Topaz, rose Quartz, Rhodonite

Working with ascended masters

Jesus, mother Therese, Aine, mother Mary, Quan Yin

Raphael, the archangel of the Heart Chakra

Archangel Raphael is the archangel who oversees healing, the doctor of the heaven.

Whit his guidance, you can remember, align your energy, and learn how to use your inner gifts to heal yourself and help others to heal.

Raphael helps us to resolve love conflicts with people that we appreciate. Also, he helps us for safe traveling. Quiet your mind, listen to your heart, follow your intuition and Raphael will be there to guide you with the kind of healing you need.

You can use the following guided meditation to work with archangel Rafael in order to balance your heart chakra:

"Close your eyes, calm down your breathing by inhaling and exhaling deeply. Imagine now, that you are surrounded by an intense emerald light.

Archangel Raphael come next to you and covered you opening your heart.

You feel the presence of the angels in the middle of your breasts, where your thymus gland is. Archangel Raphael tells you that the inner healer is within you and you have the ability to heal your body.

Start to scan your body and see what part needs healing. Now archangel Raphael encourages you to spread healing green light to that part of your body, and then to the rest of your cells. All your body blooms with this green light and presence of Raphael.

Just be sure to act upon the guidance you receive!"

Affirmation to use as mantra to balance your heart chakra

"Love is the answer to everything in life, and I give and receive love without effort and unconditionally. I am a magnet for love. I welcome love into my heart and into my life."

5. Throat Chakra - I speak

The throat chakra is the fifth chakra, and its energy is based on the Sound/Ether element. This chakra is found at level of the throat, just at the center of the neck, that's why the name used. This is your point of communication, expression, listening, creativity, vibration, speak your truth, contact with your spiritual team.

At this point, you hear God, the Supreme Energy and you can establish contact with your inner guru. The throat chakra is related to your inner truth, your life purpose, and how you communicate it with others. The throat chakra is also associated with the etheric body. Since this point, we can open other kinds of connection with the different bodies of yourself.

The essential concerns related with the throat chakra are communication, expression, speaking and hearing the truth, spontaneity.

The body parts related with the throat chakra are neck, throat, face and ears. On this energetic center, the thyroid and parathyroid gland regulate body temperature and metabolism.

Principal enemy: blame other for our situation, not being responsible for our actions

Color: Baby blue

Essential characteristics of the throat chakra are:

- Speak your truth
- Communicate with others and yourself respecting who you are
- Connect with the higher realm through your angel and spiritual team
- Get inspired and creative, and share those gifts to others
- Be able to share your voice through singing or speaking in public
- Manifesting your projects
- Commitment with your goals

Signs of an imbalanced throat chakra

- Speaking too much or inadequately
- Do not care what others say
- Being scared to speak in public
- Do not tell others the truth, lying too much
- Being excessively closed in sharing with others
- Being shy to express yourself
- Do not have idea about your life purpose
- Do not being able to connect with higher realms
- Do not being able to meditate or singing mantras
- Not being able to listen to others

Here are some *questions to ask yourself.* Answer them honestly to check blockage in your fifth chakra:

1. Is it difficult for you to express and communicate what you are thinking?
2. Do you have difficulties in communicating with others?
3. Do you feel nervous when you try to express your point of view?
4. Are you aggressive when someone does not share your opinion?
5. Does your voice frequently cracks when you talk to others? Or on important meetings?
6. Do you have swollen lymph nodes in your neck?
7. Do you act contrary to your thoughts and feelings?
8. Do you suffer from hypo or hyperthyroidism?
9. Are you a shy person?
10. Are you the person who support others when talking, but not being able to speak out to express yourself?
11. Do you constantly feel ignored when you want to add a point of view?
12. Do you feel anxious when it's your turn to speak?

13. Do you feel paralyzed before and during any public presentation?
14. Do you have ear problems?
15. Do you develop regular sinus, throat or upper respiratory infections?

How to balance the throat chakra

- Let flow your feelings: cry, yell, laugh, etc.
- Speak the truth: don't lie or exaggerate
- Meditation and inner silence
- Do not criticize or have judgment for others
- Look a blue sky, a day with no clouds
- Sing
- Sing mantras
- Use your voice to send love
- Journal
- Play music

Herbs and foods for throat chakra

- Eat a plant-based diet, mostly fruits
- Drink herbal teas made with bayberry, chamomile, peppermint, red clover, with lemon and honey, coconut water
- Eat blue food as: blueberries and blackberries

Essential oils for throat chakra

Black Pepper, Chamomile, Coriander, Cypress, Eucalyptus, Geranium, Lavender, Myrrh, Rosemary, Sage, Thyme, Yarrow

Crystals for throat chakra

Aquamarine, blue Calcite, blue Lace Agate, blue Topaz, Chalcedony, Chrysocolla, Lapiz Lazuli, Turquoise

Working with ascended masters

Jesus, Moses, Babaji, Yogananda, Pele

Gabriel, the archangel of the throat chakra

Traditionally Archangel Gabriel is the messenger of God. His name means 'God is my Strength.' He is the one who announces the incarnation of the souls, and the one who is when the newborn makes his first apparition in the world of Pachamama. He is the angel of little children, and the one who helps parents to grow and educate them. Gabriel also nourishes and supports with love our inner child. Nowadays, there are many techniques for healing the inner child. Call upon Gabriel before and during your healing sessions.

He has so many missions, between those we have: the Chief Ambassador to Humanity, the Angel of Revelation, the Bringer of Good News, Hope and Mercy.

Gabriel helps you to find the inner wisdom that resides within you, so you can be able to live and express your truth. He can also support you while you look for your life purpose and your unique inner gifts, and how you can share it with others. He also helps you to connect with and use your intuition; paying attention to it and acting with your own wisdom.

You can use the following prayer to work with archangel Gabriel in order to balance your throat chakra:

"Archangel Gabriel, I ask for your presence as I would like to communicate lovely, clearly with people around me. I also ask you for connection with my spiritual helpers. Please guide to be inspired, so I can create and share my creations to others. Please teach me how to be serene, so I can use powerful thoughts with no ego criteria. And please guide me to be a channel of the angels love and share with others your message. Thank you, Gabriel.

Affirmation to use as mantra to balance your throat chakra

"My thoughts and ideas come from a place of love. My mind is clear, and my channels of divine communication are always active to share heavenly messages. I now fully accept the wisdom, insight, and protection of my angels."

6. Third Eye - I see

The third eye chakra is the sixth chakra, and its energy is based on the Light element. The third eye chakra is found on the forehead, between the eyebrows. This is your point of intuition, vision, visualization, imagination, foresight, clarity of mind, meditation and psychic abilities. Your third eye depends on your imagination for a correct activity. Thought this point, you are able to see with your eye's soul others aspect beyond the third dimension. When you awaken and develop your third eye, you awake and work with your psychic gifts and intuition. In this point, you are able to perceive the Universe with divine vision.

The essential concerns related with the third eye chakra are: vision, intuition, memory, clairvoyance, psychic abilities and imagination.

The body parts are related with the third eye chakra are eyes and the base of the crane. On this energetic center, the pineal gland regulates biorhythms in your body, including sleep and wake time.

Principal enemy: Illusion, to be in the moon, to believe we are only light not seeing or agreeing the teaching of the darkness

Color: indigo

Essential characteristics of the third eye chakra are:

- Vision
- Intuition
- Ability to concentrate and meditate
- Able to perceive other dimensions
- Connected with your intuition and inner wisdom
- Work or being gifted with psychic abilities, specially clairvoyance and clairaudience
- Being able to see the lessons of the challenges
- Inspire and motivate others

Signs of an imbalanced third eye chakra

- Problems in eyes
- Experience headaches and migraines
- Lack of discipline
- Procrastinating instead of following goals
- Psychic fantasies and illusions, lack of grounding
- Not being able to concentrate or to focus
- Being forgetful, confused and lack of insight
- Not being able to get inspired and to create
- Being psychosomatic and create illness from anywhere
- Having nightmares
- Being superstitious
- Worrying a lot

- Experience depression
- Experience anger

Here are some *questions to ask yourself*. Answer them honestly to check blockage in your sixth chakra:

1. Do you have headaches and/or migraines?
2. Are you creating illness or being afraid to get sick?
3. Do you have difficulty to get grounded?
4. Do you experience mood disorders?
5. Do you find yourself competing often with others?
6. Do you have poor memory?
7. Are you not being inspired and creative?
8. Is your imagination diminishing?
9. Are you addicted to social events?
10. Are you not being focused to finish one task?

How to balance the third eye chakra

- Let yourself feel your emotions
- Develop and understand your limitations
- Meditation
- Yoga
- Visualization
- Listen your inner voice, your intuition
- Forgiveness
- Gratitude
- Work your negative beliefs
- Watch the sky full of starts
- Concentrate and focus only in one task at the time
- Repeat positive affirmation to improve your health

Herbs and foods for third eye chakra

- Use these herbs as teas or room spray: mint, star anise, got kola, dill, thyme, rosemary, juniper, poppy seed, valerian, mugwort
- Eat carrots to improve your vision. Also take supplements as vitamin B complex, vitamin B12, lutein, and/or vitamin D3
- Eat purple and blue foods like red onion, red cabbage, blueberries, red cabbage, aubergine, figs, juneberries, plums, red grapes, blackberries, raspberries, raisins, and eggplant
- Consider seaweed (rich in iodine), kale, spinach, broccoli, almonds, oranges, flax and sesame seeds, and any chlorophyll

- Consider red wines, grape juice and organic apple cider vinegar

Essential oils for third eye chakra

Angelica Seed, Basil, Bergamot, black Pepper, Carrot Seed, Clary Sage, Clove Bud, Frankincense, Ginger, Holy Basil, Jasmine, Lavender, Lemon, Melissa, Mint, Peppermint, Pine, Orange, Rosemary, Rosewood

Crystals for third eye chakra

Blue Calcite - Iolite - Lapis Lazuli - Saphire - Sodalite - Sugilite - Tanzanite

Working with ascended masters

Ashtar, Buddha, Jesus, Sanat Kumara, Solomon

Michael, the archangel of the Third Eye Chakra

Archangel Michael is probably the most famous of all the archangels. Usually he's painted with his sword and shield, indicating his ability to protect and to eliminate ego and fear.

He has so many roles. Here are some of Michael's main roles:

Protection

Michael is the personification of strength and valor. He is involved in protecting any aspect of your being, including physical, spiritual and mental bodies. He also protects your belongings and honor.

Protection while in you are in your car

Michael diffuses protection while you are driving in your car. I normally call upon him in any journey including the short ones that I take in my car.

Protection of your belongings

Archangel Michael watch over your personal property and anything you own. Ask for his help when you feel unprotected about your belongings in any way.

Spiritual Protection

Archangel Michael is the higher protector of any kind, including the one related to energy. Most of the times, we are not able to see these energies, but most of you can feel when your energy is affected. You can feel tired or sad. You've probably identified people or situations when it does happen. Call upon Michael to protect your spirit and keep your energy to work for your dreams.

Protecting Job and Reputation

Archangel Michael is an excellent helper with work issues and protect us in any situation related to keep and improve our job. You can call upon him for help when you want to have a better position and when you want to keep the reputation of your job.

Life-Purpose

Archangel Michael knows your soul purpose and soul plan. He knows what your inner gifts are, and the direction you should take in order to remember and use them. He guides you to make changes and take actions to embrace your sacred and unique path, so you can live your life purpose.

You can use the following prayer to work with archangel Michael in order to balance your third eye chakra:

"Dear Archangel Michael, please surround me, please protect my beloved ones and me from any kind of insecurity. Please be my sword and my shield to be untouchable by any being who does not respect my higher self. Please guide me to embrace my inner unique gifts and live my life purpose and sacred path."

Affirmation to use as mantra to balance your root chakra

"I now know, accept, act and see following my inner guide, living fully my life mission in this planet. I understand and embrace my sacred path. I am tuned with the higher energy of the Creator and the eternal wisdom of the Universe."

7. Crown Chakra - I know

The crown chakra is the seventh chakra, and its energy is based on the

Thought/Knowing element. The seventh chakra is found at the top of the head in the area of our crown. This is your point of divine connection, divine wisdom, consciousness, knowledge, information, meditation, humanity, giving to others and spiritual love. The activity of this chakra is based on your awareness and consciousness getting in touch with the infinite wisdom of the Universe. This is the point where you open a portal of connection with the universal consciousness.

The essential concerns related with the crown chakra are: connection to the divinity, to your guides and angels, to your subconscious, to your inner wisdom, divine guidance, and enlightenment.

The body parts related with the crown chakra are the nervous system, cerebral cortex, and endocrine system. On this energetic center, the pituitary gland produces hormones and governs the function of the previous five glands.

Principal enemy: attachment

Color: violet

Essential characteristics of the crown chakra are:

- Consciousness
- Awareness
- Wisdom
- Sacredness
- Connection with the Spirit or Divinity
- Communication with higher realms
- Connection with your angel and spiritual team
- Setting free from restrictive archetypes
- Bliss, rapture and joy

Signs of an imbalanced crown chakra

- Being disconnected to spirit or divinity
- Not being able to ground, living constantly on the moon
- Right eye problems
- Neurological or/and nervous system disorder
- Loss of direction in life and/or life purpose
- Lack of faith and hope
- Being disconnected with your physical body paying only attention to your higher chakras

- Obsession with spiritual work and your super powers
- Mental disorder as: addictions, schizophrenia, bipolar, dementia, multiple personality disorders, attention deficit
- Not being able to manage stress and worries

Here are some *questions to ask yourself.* Answer them honestly to check blockage in your seventh chakra:

1. Is it difficult for you to be grounded?
2. Do you live more in the moon than on Earth? Do you have illusions most of the time?
3. Do you have difficulty to accept limitations and challenges?
4. Are you able to detach yourself from people or situations?
5. Are you lost on your life purpose?
6. Is it difficult for you to believe in what your eyes can not see?
7. Do you constantly ask others their opinion about how to resolve your challenges?
8. Do you easily become distracted or lose focus on what you are doing?
9. Do you finish what you've started?
10. Do you believe in the existence of a divine Creator? Not matter what you name it?
11. Do you believe or practice any philosophy of the existence of life?
12. Do you experience lack of inspiration?
13. Is it difficult for you to accept oth opinion? Do you want to be right most of the time?
14. Do your limiting beliefs control you?
15. Are you extremist with your religion or beliefs?

How to balance the crown chakra

- Surrender
- Respect life, Universe and other forms of existence
- Meditation
- Be one with the planet and others
- Acceptance
- Gratitude
- Rituals to connect with your inner god/goddess
- Be in a high mountain
- Look at the sky
- Yoga postures like Shavasana or Lotus position

Herbs and foods for root chakra

- Detoxifying and cleanse of your body
- Fasting
- Eat purple and blue foods like red onion, red cabbage, blueberries, red cabbage, aubergine, figs, juneberries, plums, red grapes, blackberries, raspberries, raisins, and eggplant
- Food for your brain as: fatty fish, caffeine, turmeric, broccoli, dark chocolate, pumpkin seeds, nuts, oranges, eggs, green tea

Essential oils for crown chakra

Cedarwood, Elemi, Frankincense, Jasmine, Linden Blossom, Melissa, Myhrr, Neroli, Rose, Rosemary, Rosewood, Violet Leaf, Water Lily, Ylang Ylang

Crystals for crown chakra

Amethyst, Chariote, Clear Quartz, Selenite

Working with ascended masters

Jesus, Moses, Solomon

Zadkiel, the archangel of the crown chakra

Archangel Zadkiel is a great helper for your memory, especially when you need assistance for exams or tests. He also helps you to remember your divine origin, your soul mission and why you are in this planet. Being the angel of compassion, he will help you to feel it in your heart, so you can forgive and accept others as they are. He is a great healer of past memories from this life and past lives.

Archangel Zadkiel can help you to transmute your energies, so you can change from a victim role to a 'creator's role. He can help you to activate the violet flame and transform what you need to rebuild at that time of your soul's path. Zadkiel helps us to remember that we all are children of God, the Creator, and there is no need for competition. We all come from the same source and we all go to the same source of eternal love.

You can use the following prayer to work with archangel Zadkiel in order to balance your crown chakra:

"Archangel Zadkiel, please help me heal my heart. Help me to understand other's life with not criticizing but just feeling compassion. Please help me to accept others and accept my path, so I can welcome joy and bliss in my life. Help me to embrace my inner gifts and see other one's gifts, recognizing that there is divinity in every person. Help my heart to feel forgiveness and apply it to anyone that hurt me in the past. Help me to set myself free, so I can follow my life's path and my soul's evolution."

Affirmation to use as mantra to balance your crown chakra

"I am complete and ONE with the Divine Energy. I now fully accept the wisdom, insight, connection with the Universe. I now accept to be a bridge between the stars and the earth."

☐

CHAPTER 8: HEALING WITH THE ANGELS

Through the assistance of God and angels, any condition can be healed, while increasing health and energy to promote a healthy lifestyle. To do so, the person must surrender to God and the angels' assistance; must believe that healing is possible and that their celestial team is working already on healing their body, mind and spirit. It's important to understand that Angel Healing does not interfere with any religious or spiritual beliefs. The presence of the angels has a calming effect on people inducing them to relax, to soothe, and to find peace.

What is Angel Healing or Angel therapy?

Doreen Virtue defines 'Angel Therapy' as a type of alternative therapy which actually includes a non-denominational spiritual method of healing and involves the chore of communicating and working with the guardian angels and archangels to heal various health problems including the physical, mental and spiritual health. Angel therapy can be applied to any area of your life, including health, love, relationships, work, abundance, etc.

Angelic Healing helps to clean and clear energies, release blockages, fears and traumas, refresh you with soul stamina, healing on different levels: physical, emotional, spiritual, and mentally. Sometimes our energy system gets blocked due to low energies from feeling anger, fear, pain, resentment or anything that is not in true alignment with who we are. In this case, angel healing helps us to feel more in balance with the essence of our being. We discover that we can follow our soul path and our life purpose!

With this kind of healing, the angels works with the therapist guiding while he/she is performing the session. The therapist becomes a channel or a vessel for the angels letting himself or herself be guided by the celestial healing team. This energy will cleanse and clear; allowing the client to recharge himself or herself during the session.

The angels can help us to remove any blockage in our bodies and bring back your state of being. That is your divine right. The client co-works with the therapist trusting and having faith in the angels and also his or her own abilities to heal. Faith and trusting are crucial factors on the healing session.

What are the angels associated with healing purposes?

The Archangel associated with healing is Archangel Raphael, assisted by other Healing Angels. Raphael's energy is color green. He and the Healing Angels can assist you to choose healthy food and overcoming addictions. Your illness can be treated anywhere: examples at your place, at a hospital. They can assist you when a health emergency occurs or during time of recovery.

I always visualize Archangel Raphael and his emerald green light coming next to the person needing healing. I visualize the doctor covered by Raphael's energy, so he embodies the doctor or person who is going to touch the patient. Every time I go to the hospital, I feel Raphael's energy working everywhere, sending the Healing Angels where they are needed to be.

Raphael and the Healing Angels act also as our health coach inspiring in us, ideas to increase our vitality, encouraging us to practice exercises and motivate us to find techniques to reduce stress, and raise your energy and self-esteem. They become your best guides to teach you a healthy lifestyle. Just ask for their help when you are inspired to take care of the beautiful soul's temple that is your body. Angels encourage you to spend time outdoors so you can refresh and energize yourself through the renewing energy of trees, fresh air, water, sunshine, and nature as a whole. Work with them!

How to perform Angelic Healing?

Everybody can perform Angelic Healing. The angels love to work with anyone who follows a regular practice of prayer. That's why your daily practice with your celestial team is very important to enhance the relationship.

You can start doing your own healing sessions and then incorporating sessions on your friends or people in need. The sessions can be made at any place convenient for this type of healing: your place, at the place of the person looking for healing. The most important feature is to find a quiet space where you are not going to be interrupted or distracted. Turn your cell phones off, play an angelic melody, burn incense, light a green or white candle, and grab your crystals or items you will use during the session.

Center yourself and make sure you are aligned with the angelic realm. Start by invoking Raphael and the Healing Angels, visualizing an emerald green light surrounding the person who will be healed: yourself or a second party. Feel the energy of the person; scan it, letting it guide you to the body region which needs special attention. It's possible during the meditation to receive instructions to stay in one part of the body; passing energy. You could also receive an instruction to work with a particular kind of crystal. Just flow with the session; being a channel for healing. You can also use aromatherapy to strengthen the efficacy of the healing session.

From your heart chakra, you can visualize a green and pink light going to all the parts of the body of the person in need, and from them you can even visualize the cells and atoms receiving this energy. Remember the body is a system. You cannot be sick in one part of your body and not be in the rest. Your blood becomes a river, the river of life. You can visualize that this green and pink energy travels through this river bringing the nectar of life everywhere.

If you are working with another person, please ask before the session if you can touch some parts of their bodies during the session. You can work just placing your hands some inches above the person. It's not necessary in all cases to touch the person. However, in some cases I have received the instruction to press some points of the person to activate certain energetic channels. But it's not always the case. Just be sure to not intimidate the person who came for healing assistance.

Will I see angels during the session?

Many people get anxious about seeing angels even get scared to see them during the session. You need to know that not everyone has the same gifts or spiritual abilities to see them. There are some people who develop one psychic sensitivity corresponding to the senses: clairvoyance (clear vision), clairaudience (clear audio/hearing), clairsentience (clear sensation or feeling), clairscent (clear smelling), clairtangency (clear touching), clairgustance (clear tasting), and clairempathy (clear emotion). Other people develop more than one psychic sensitivity. There is no rule for everyone.

Every soul is so unique and different. Sometimes we come to the session or angelic practices with expectations. With all my love, let me tell you something: leave your expectations behind. Embrace your own gifts and enjoy them. Come to the practice with an open heart and an open mind. If you see them, it's wonderful. If you do not see them, it's wonderful too. Probably you will discover other psychic sense and enjoy the ride. No matter what your gift is; angel healing is effective for everyone who trusts!

What can I feel during the session?

The feelings are diverse: some people feel the energy flow, some feel warmth, some feel lighter or elevated, some might feel a tingling, and some don't feel anything. Just be ready to receive the healing that you need in divine time and divine order. Raphael and the Healing Angels know exactly what you need now. Just do your homework and trust!!

What happens after the session?

Usually, people feel free of a charge or blockages. They feel liberated and a change of energy. I always tell my clients to drink water to help the healing and releasing what was removed during the session. I also tell them that they might feel tired, need a nap, or make time for a rest. Let the healing take place and let it settle in your entire system.

Angel Healing helps you to feel more balanced, cleansed, free, liberated, energized, restored, and healed on a physical, emotional, and spiritual level.

Should I leave my medical treatment?

Medical conditions can be treated with Angel Therapy. However, it is NOT a substitute for medical treatment. Both can work together for a better result on healing. Please consult a healthcare professional if you have any serious illnesses or psychiatric problems.

This alternative therapy can be combined with therapies like crystal therapy, aromatherapy, sound therapy, as effective healing technique for eradicating spiritual blockage or extreme negativity causing you physical illness.

Following, I share some techniques of Angel Healing/Angel Therapy which I use with my clients. You can practice these techniques on yourself or on other adults, children, and even pets.

Healing Angels

The archangel associated with healing is Archangel Raphael, assisted by the other Healing Angels. However, all the archangels perform healing assistance with particular issues detailed above. It's known that angels and archangels work with us 24 hours a day during your entire lifetime. However, every archangel's energy is associated with a particular day. Below, you will find the best day to work with the energy of every archangel and the colors working with their energy.

Ariel

Day	Tuesday
Color	Pale Pink
Good for healing	animals, the natural world, relieve infections, helps to heal problems with the back, blood circulation, heart. He also helps us to regenerate from the states of anxiety and stress.

Azrael

Day	Tuesday
Color	Creamy white
Good for healing	Colon problems, hemorrhoids, tendons, muscles, bones. He also helps us with hyper sensitivity, melancholy, apathy, or even terminal illness.

Chamuel

Day	Friday
Color	Pink
Good for healing	blood, fatigue, bone, and joint disorders, burns, cuts, wounds, fevers, blood pressure—high and low, and problems with anger or aggression.

Gabriel

Day	Monday
Color	Baby blue or white
Good for healing	hormonal imbalance, menstrual and menopausal problems, balances all bodily fluids, restores harmony with our natural reproductive cycles, the reproductive system and fertility, including the production of sperm, the kidneys and bladder, biorhythms, and sleep problems.

Haniel

Day	Monday and Friday
Color	Bluish white
Good for healing	lymphatic system, asthma, allergic issues, sciatic nerve, arteries, water retention and any problems related with the breast, brain, and digestive system.

Jeremiel

Day	Tuesday
Color	Purple
Good for healing	respiratory problems, ear problems, difficulties in pregnancy. He also helps us dealing with stress, and to take an important decision based on our discernment and intuition.

Jophiel

Day	Friday
Color	Yellow
Good for healing	nervous system, dry mouth, varicose veins, bones and muscles problems, hyperthyroid, cellulitis, frigidity, vocal cords problems. Jophiel helps us to renew our cells and regenerate them.

Metatron

Day	Monday
Color	White and pink with green swirls
Good for healing	children, cardiovascular, neurological, endocrine and nervous system, immune problems, promoting healthy bones, giving energy.

Michael

Day	Sunday
Color	Royal blue
Good for healing	immune system, all neurological conditions, viruses and infections that do not clear, whole body, mind, and spirit healing, brain and personality disorders, good for overcoming feelings of alienation from life or obsession with perfection.

Raphael

Day	Wednesday
Color	Emerald green
Good for healing	any major health problems, when needing surgery, before and after medical tests and any necessary prolonged chemical or X-ray treatments; helps digestion, liver, spleen, gall, bladder, stomach and small intestine, abdomen, back, muscles, pancreas, adrenal glands, autonomic nerve system, and the metabolism. He also helps with self-confidence and counteracts hyperactivity and workaholic tendencies.

Raguel

Day	Wednesday
Color	Pale blue
Good for healing	food problems (especially when you have troubles to balance your nutritional needs). Raguel helps us to digest what is hard for us to process in our life. Raguel helps us dealing with menopause and stammering.

Raziel

Day	Wednesday
Color	Rainbow
Good for healing	pain especially headache and migraines, the effect of traumas or abuse, assists the management of lifelong or hereditary conditions. He is very helpful to work on our pineal gland and problems related to thyroid, back pain, heart.

Sandalphon

Day	Friday
Color	Turquoise
Good for healing	problems related with neck and throat. Sandalphon is also good helping with issues related to the heart, infections or contagious illness, blood circulation, constipation, and bladder.

Uriel

Day	Thursday
Color	Ruby and gold
Good for healing	lower back, hips, legs, knees, and feet, bowels including the large intestine, the anus, prostate gland, and genitals. He is a good helper for IBS, celiac disease, and constipation, nail splitting, and panic attacks or irritability.

Zadkiel

Day	Saturday
Color	Violet and lilac
Good for healing	rheumatoid and neuralgic issues, sleeping problems, issues related to pancreas, kidney, sclerosis, lymphatic system, intoxication, stress and anxiety.

Healing Crystals

You can use crystals associated with archangels and the specific aspect desired to heal. Just remember to make a little invocation before starting the healing session to give the intention to the crystals and the angels.

Example of Invocation:

"Divine Healing Angels and spirits elementals of the crystal (say the name of the crystal you are working with), I call upon you now. Please assist, guide and protect me for healing. I ask for your help on healing (express the health condition or emotional condition you want to work on.) Please bring wisdom to my inner being, so I can understand the lesson and embrace health as my divine right. Thank you."

On the following chart, you will find crystals associated to specific illness conditions. Grab a crystal depending on the issue you need to work. If your intuition tells you to grab another crystal, please trust your intuition. I believe your intuition is very powerful, and we heal when we trust. You need to trust your intuition! This is only a guide for you:

Healing with Crystals: Physical Illness			
Healing focus	**Crystal**	**Healing focus**	**Crystal**
Adictions	Aventurine	Headache	Amethyst, Sugilite
Allergies	Chrysocolla	Heart	Peridot
Anxiety	Citrine, Lapis Lazuli	Immune System	Blue Quartz, Malachite
Arthritis	Cooper, Smokey Quartz	Infection	Ruby, Turquoise
Asthma	Rhodonite	Joints	Hematite
Back	Blue Calcite	Kidneys	Carnelian, Jade
Bladder	Carnelian	Legs	Jade
Blood	Carnelian	Liver	Azurite, Malachite, Peridot
Bones	Calcite	Lungs	Chrysocolla
Breast	Amethyst, Peridot	Menopause	Garnet, Lapis Lazuli, Moonstone
Broken Heart	Malachite, Rose Quartz	Menstrual Period	Moonstone, Smokey Quartz
Cancer	Rhodocrosite	Migraines	Tourmaline
Circulation	Citrine, Pyrite	Nails	Calcite, Opal, Pearl
Colds	Fluorite	Ovaries	Tiger's Eye, Moonstone
Colon	Amber, Malachite	Pain	Malachite, Sugilite
Diabetis	Amethyst, Jasper, Malachite	Pancreas	Green Moss Agate
Ears	Amber, Blue Fluorite	Skin	Azurite, Malachite
Eyes	Aquamarine, Rhodocrosite	Teeth	Calcite, Fluorite
Feet	Aquamarine, Onyx	Throat	Amber, Tourmaline, Turquoise
Gallbladder	Garnet, Jasper	Thyroid	Chrysocolla, Tiger's Eye, Pyrite
Genitals	Garnet, Obsidian	Urinary Tract	Amber, Citrine, Jade
Hair	Malachite, Opal, Quartz	Veins	Aquamarine, Opal
Hands	Quartz		

Angel Therapy Techniques

In this section, I share techniques used on angel medicine to help us to achieve a healthy life. I repeat again, there is no a magic or strict formula to do them. You can add or take out things that do not resonate with you. Here, I share what has been working for my clients and me.

Cutting cords with archangel Michael

Everything in this universe is connected energetically. Everyone on this planet has etheric cords or psychic cords with other people. These energy cords are connecting one person to another and making genuine connections between each other. The energy cords become a pathway interconnecting emotions and thoughts between the beings involved.

When we have these cords, we share the same vibrational energy and get frequency from the other person and vice versa. Sometimes these cords are responsible for unexplained pain or discomfort due to the charge of energy. They are based, in some cases, on fear-based or attachment or lower feelings.

When we connect with people in our lives, they can be charged on different energy levels. It's important to understand that cutting cords is not abandoning the other person; it's just releasing the unhealthy part of the relationship.
Archangel Michael is the best helper for cutting cords. He has a sword that can assist you cutting etheric cords.

For this exercise, find a quiet place where you won't be disturbed. If you have some candles, light it and focus on your breathing until you feel yourself entering into a meditative state. Scan your body and feel anywhere that is tight. Pay attention to the energy, the colors during your meditative state, the temperature. You will sense in your body where this cord could be placed. Picture the cord as a physical connection and then imagine Archangel Michael with his 'Indigo light' cutting through it. Imagine cutting cords over and over again. You will start to feel lighter and lighter during the exercise. Repeat the exercise until you find your body relaxed.

It is possible that during the treatment, you receive information about the origin of the cords. You could hear the name of the person which you have established the cord, you can remember the place where it happened, you can smell a fragrance of some flowers, or any clue related to the cord that will help you to understand the nature of it and will help you to release it with unconditional love.

While you are cutting the cords with the help of Archangel Michael, you can say a prayer to him. There is no a magic formula for this. Follow your intuition and let yourself be guided to him. Below is one model you can use:

"Archangel Michael, I call upon you for assistance. I ask for your guide and assistance in cutting cords that no longer serves me. At this moment of my life, it's difficult for me to break these cords by myself. I ask for your assistance to align my energy with love and light, in order to free both parties from these recurring negative energies. Thank you."

Cutting addiction

Addictions are distractions for your spiritual path and your life purpose. These addictions can be related to substances, food, beverages, unhealthy behaviors and even relationships. They become a vice cycle keeping you away from living a balanced and healthy life. Cutting these cords will make you feel better and align with your higher inner self. Addiction actions bring sadness, guilty, shame, emptiness, rage and even depression into your life. With these acts, you hurt yourself, you blame yourself, you criticize yourself, living constantly judged by the worst judge: yourself. When you are able to cut this vice cycle, you are able to create a new reality and optional story very different from the unhealthy reality that you are living.

Archangel Raphael is the archangel who can help us cutting addictive cords. He wants to support you on your life purpose and soul mission towards a healthy life where you reach your goals and dreams.

For this exercise, find a quiet place where you won't be disturbed. If you have some candles, light it and focus on your breathing until you feel yourself entering into a meditative state. Now visualize the foods, substances, beverages that you would like to release. See them in front of you at the level of your belly button saying, for example: "Archangel Raphael, please release from me any addiction cords so I can live a balanced and healthy life now."

You can feel a white light cleansing your aura and cutting addictions from you. Ask archangel Raphael to send his energy so that you feel protected from any cravings: For example: "Archangel Raphael, please send your emerald green light to surround my mind, and my stomach to prevent any cravings or desires for unhealthy choices in the future. Thank you."

Removing negativity by vacuuming with Archangel Michael

During our lifetime, we could have absorbed negative energy coming from our own fear or from others' people energetic field. This energy can make you feel tired, sad, or no motivation with no forces. Sometimes we can deal with challenging relationships than weaken your energetic field and we accumulate what I call 'energetic dirt.' The following technique is done with the help of archangel Michael.

For this exercise, find a quiet place where you won't be disturbed. If you have some candles, light it and focus on your breathing until you feel yourself entering into a meditative state. Now visualize yourself in peace, and in front of archangel Michael. You can say a short prayer like this: "Archangel Michael, I need your assistance to clear my energy using your celestial vacuum."

You can feel archangel Michael passing the vacuum tube starting by your crown chakra (top of your head) and continue through your body. Follow your intuition; at this moment you are working with archangel Michael, guiding him in any area you feel there is 'energetic dirt.' Be sure to get to all the areas of your body and stay longer when you feel the 'energetic dirt' is adhered.

If you feel there is something heavy, call upon the angels of protection to help you take that heavy energy out of your system. While you are doing this process, you can pray to archangel Michael or repeat a powerful mantra. You can also say: "Michael, please remove what is not love outside of me."

This technique is powerful as an energetic cleanse. Be sure to drink water after it, wash your hands, and send love to the energy removed and know that is no longer in your system.

This is very helpful when you are dealing with sadness, depression, lack of motivation in your life. Try it; give yourself a gift of a soul cleansed.

Removing Vows

Vows are sacred words and promises that we make to the Great Spirit or Divine Creator. Generally, they involve our agreement from our soul to others and God. A soul is always loyal to the commitments made, and it will always try to respect these vows. However, these 'sacred promises of the past' may have been carried through many past lives right into our life now.

Some of these vows are not helping us, and probably blocking our path of manifestation, in this lifetime. For example: you do not understand why you do attract love relationships that don't work or last; you may attract situations that block your prosperity; you do not understand why everything is so hard to achieve or overcome in your life.

With some practice you can cut this vows and get rid of the past life baggage. Remember, your soul always respects the lesson chosen before incarnation and will always want you to be a free spirit.

The purpose of the following exercise is to undo any vows carried from a past life; holding you back on the achievement of your dreams.

For this, work with archangel Michael to enhance the power of breaking the vows and try to do it on a Full Moon to attract the powerful energy of this magical element.

- (If you desire) Light a candle and incense, creating a sacred space to start the ritual.
- Call upon the four directions Fire (candle), Water, Earth (crystals or salt), and Air (with incense or smudge).
- Sit down and relax. Enter in a state of complete relaxation. Do some breathing exercises— inhaling slowly and exhaling slowly.
- Meditate on what kind of vows you need to work on. It can happen that we could have made vows of: chastity, celibacy, self-abnegation, separation, obedience, sacrifice, poverty, silence... Ask your heart which one(s) apply to you.
- Call upon archangel Michael and ask for help to break the vows:

For example: "Archangel Michael, please bring your celestial and protective energy to my space. I ask your help to break these vows that are no longer serving me in this lifetime. I ask for your protection and help to release what no longer is good for me in my life. I want to embrace life with all the gifts that I deserve. Thank you."

- Now please repeat three times the following prayer proposed by healpastlives.com for every kind of vow you are working with:

"In the past, I made a vow of (name the type of vow you have made). I acknowledge the lesson of this vow. Now I realize that this vow no longer serves me. I now release this old vow from my energetic body, my unconsciousness level and my consciousness level. I release any limitations that has been blocked me until now. I embrace a new vow of (name your new vow) and bring it completely to my whole existence. I ask my spiritual helpers and guides to bring these new energies into my life, opening my heart to receive new divine and material gifts. I embrace change and the richness carried by a new wave of energy. So be it, it is so."

You can also create your own prayer to break any vows.

- Give thanks to the Divine Creator, archangel Michael, and yourself.

Healing Temple

Use the following meditation to connect with the healing frequency of archangel Raphael and the Healing Angels. You can create this healing chamber; when you need healing assistance for yourself, family and friends.

You can use crystals in any green tones, specially Malachite or green emerald to support you in this exercise.

- (If you desire) Light a candle or incense and play angelical music.
- Close your eyes and take some very deep breaths; visualizing three beings with white light in front of you. These light beings love you very much and you feel their unconditional, nonjudgmental love pouring over you.

They take you by your hands, and you will allow them to guide you. You look down and notice that the three are floating over in the air. They guide you to a beautiful place in the forest; full of trees; and animals that live in harmony. You take a deep breath and feel that the air is pure; bringing oxygen into the organs of your body.

You continue walking, and this time you perceive in the distance a crystal temple. The three light beings are walking with you, and you feel secured and protected to do this journey with them.
When you arrive to this temple, you perceive a green light shining inside the temple. Immediately, you hear a warm voice inviting you to come to a crystal bed. This voice introduces himself as Archangel Raphael and asks you to lie down and breathe deeply to help the oxygen collaborate during the healing session.
Archangel Raphael stays at the top of your head and the three light beings place themselves on the other three directions of the bed covering totally your body.

Archangel Raphael asks your permission to start scanning your different bodies. Once the permission is given, green healing light enters into your body; reaching all the organs and cells. (Stay here as long as you need.)

- Once the session is complete, archangel Raphael seals your heart and your thymus area to strength your immune system. You leave the temple in harmony, surrounded by the three light beings, that bring you through the forest and finally to your inner self.

- Come back to the room and drink plenty of water. Write down how you feel after the session in the Healing Temple.

For better results, you can record this meditation with your own voice. Allow yourself just to relax while you hear yourself guiding you in this exercise.

Healing your inner child

Use the following meditation to connect with the healing frequency of archangel Metatron and the Healing Angels. The energy of Metatron contains high frequency to heal the memories that remain in our consciousness and unconsciousness regarding our path as a child.

It's necessary to understand that all human beings were a pure child; and we still are these pure beings on God's eyes. Whatever happened at that time of our life was not your fault, neither your parents. They were repeating what probably your grandparents taught them. There is no wrong in any story. We have the ability to re-create a space where we can find peace with our story; while supporting and loving this inner child that is still living within us.

You can use crystals in any pink and green tones, specially Watermelon Tourmaline to support you in this exercise.

- (If you desire) Light a candle or incense and play angelical music.
- Close your eyes and take some very deep breath visualizing YOURSELF, when you were 5 years old. If you have any remember; you can go to an earlier age. Stay in that moment watching what this innocent and pure child is doing. Take some deep breaths here.

Contemplating this beautiful scene, you realize that there is a being next to you, watching over you, spreading light everywhere you go, everywhere you play. This is Metatron, and his energy is green and pink. He is always next to you, and you can feel and hear what he is saying to you.

Now, try to go to a sad scene with your parents or a family member. Feel how you felt at that time. Where is the pain? in what part of your body? Is it your heart? Don't be afraid; it's just a memory. You are a lovely adult now, ready to take care of this beautiful child, and you are not alone. When you turn around, you can see fairies and other light beings that are next to you

166

holding you during this sad moment.

Now we are going to go deeper and see the eyes of the person who did that to you. While you see an adult, you perceive there is also a child, looking for protection, looking for love. He/she has suffered many things when he/she was a child. This is only a way to manifest the sadness of his/her heart. There's nothing wrong with you. You are a pure child as is that person who harmed you.

Now, Metatron holds your heart and asks you to express compassion towards this person in from of you. You can feel that this compassion starts to take away the pain that this situation left in your heart many years ago. Metatron now teaches you that only love can heal... and you have a lot of love in your heart. You want to heal; you want to let free your heart and decide to surround this entire situation with pink light of unconditional love. Forgiveness arises at that moment, and your heart feels liberate.
You see that everything around you is covered completely with pink light and this time you can say goodbye and I love you to the person in front of you. You have been so brave to close this cycle and Metatron is very proud of YOU.

You hug Metatron and manifest your gratitude towards this enlighten being.

- Now it's time to come back. The sadness is no longer there, and you are covered with pink and green light leaving its imprints in you. Feel blessed and proud of yourself.
- Come back to the room and drink plenty of water and write how you feel after the session on the Healing Temple.

For better results, you can record this meditation with your own voice. Allow yourself just to relax while you hear yourself guiding you in this exercise.

Healing your ancestors

Use the following meditation to connect with the healing frequency of archangel Haniel and the Healing Angels. This archangel works with the energy of the moon. You can do this exercise anytime, but it is much better near or in full moon.

Archangel Haniel oversees our relationships with our ancestral lineage and the consequences of their acts impacting our present life. You can use crystals in any white tones, especially Moonstone, to support you in this exercise.

- (If you desire) Light a candle or incense and play angelical music.
- Close your eyes and take a deep breath visualizing a full moon and a big tree with huge roots. The roots go deeper and deeper into the earth. Now, you ask permission to grandfather tree to enter inside to connect with your lineage.

Once inside, you feel a warm white light that surrounds you and encompasses your heart. This is Archangel Haniel coming to walk the path of your ancestors with you.

You are not afraid to go deeper. You know that you are not alone and have all the light you need to explore the dark area of the tree's roots.
You arrive to one of the root branches and discover your great grandmother is here waiting for you. She asks you to light a candle for her. You remember you brought candles with you, and they are in your pocket. You light a candle in honor of your great grandmother and express your love to her and all her ancestors.

She starts to show you some unpleasant patrons that are on your ancestral path. She shows you how her grandparents suffered, and her parents repeated this pattern without knowing that they can change it. She tells you she was waiting for you, so YOU can be the one that changes this behavior pattern and bring healing to your ancestors. You agree that you will do this task.

Haniel tells you, there is always one person in the family that will be the hero. This person does not reproduce the negative behavior pattern in the future generations. This person needs to be a brave warrior with no fear to break all the accumulated pain. This warrior is YOU!

Haniel guides you to touch your great grandmother's heart and send her all the light coming from your heart. Now it's time to send that light with compassion and love for all those who walked before you in your lineage. (Stay here as long as you need.)

Once this part is done, your great grandmother makes you walk to all the root branches of the tree to leave candles, at every branch, for every ancestor, living in the other dimension.
You feel in peace. You feel gratitude and love with your family and those who made possible your life today.

- Haniel lets you know that is time to come back. You say goodbye to your great grandmother. Your great grandmother expresses her gratitude. You start to go up to the center of the tree. Here you say goodbye to Haniel. He has been your guide during this trip to the roots of your ancestry.

- Come back to the room and drink plenty of water and write how you feel after the session on the Healing Temple.

For better results, you can record this meditation with your own voice. Allow yourself just to relax while you hear yourself guiding you in this exercise.

Healing past lives

Use the following meditation to connect with the healing frequency of archangel Jeremiel, archangel Raziel and the Healing Angels. Both Jeremiel and Raziel assist you when you need help to heal situations in past-lives that are causing consequences in your present life.

Archangels Jeremiel and Raziel are able to open those portals for your soul to travel to those spaces where a trauma has been caused, and still acting in your life.

You can use crystals in any purple or even the rainbow tones, especially Fluorite or Clear Quartz to support you in this exercise.

- (If you desire) Light a candle or incense and play angelical music.
- Close your eyes and take a deep breath. Visualize two beings with white light in front of you. The more you advance; you can perceive these two beings bringing you all the colors of the rainbow. They introduce themselves as archangels Jeremiel and Raziel. They hold your hands and invite you to see a rainbow in front of you. Under this rainbow dwells a portal where your soul can remember information of your past souls' adventures with other bodies.

You decide to go under and go through this portal. You arrive at a place you have been before. It can be a castle, ruins, the forest, the sea, a place with animals, a farm, and a little town. It can even be a dark place; such as a war or a battle. Feel your surroundings. Take your time to see everything around you. Take the time to smell, to perceive people, animals and your surroundings. (Stay here the time you need.)

Now that you have identified where you are; feel if there is a pain in your body and/or in your heart. What is the reason you came back to that moment? Is there something you need to solve? Is there something you need to close? Do you have to say good bye to anyone? Are you experiencing physical pain? Do you feel abandoned? Explore the cause of this pain and its lesson? (Stay here the time you need.)

Now with the help of archangel Jeremiel and Raziel, you are going to close that cycle. You will not repeat 'it' anymore in your present life. Imagine yourself in the middle of both archangels. The three of you bring your arms in front and start to send rainbow energy covering this situation completely. Feel love, feel forgiveness, feel compassion towards this situation and express gratitude to let it go. (Stay here the time you need.)

Once you have finished, the three of you hug each other. Once again, they hold your hands and bring you back to that portal of dimensions.

- Before passing through, you express gratitude to Jeremiel and Raziel for their guidance and support. Now you can return to the present.
- Come back to the room and drink plenty of water and write how do you feel after the session on the Healing Temple.

For better results, you can record this meditation with your own voice. Allow yourself just to relax while you hear yourself guiding you in this exercise.

☐

CHAPTER 9: ANGELS OF ABUNDANCE

What is abundance?

Abundance is our divine right as children of the Creator. As humans, we experience fear caused by limiting beliefs coming from our families and society. Luckily, God, the great creator, sent us celestial helpers to remind that we have the ability to create infinite possibilities of reality. One of those realities is abundance.

Abundance is not only having a lot of money but also property. Abundance refers to have plenty of health, love, ideas, time, and any other characteristic that helps us be a whole being.

Money is energy

Our planet and the Universe are composed of energy, therefore all derivatives, such as money, are a form of energy as well. We use it to exchange goods or services. What we attach to money is what we receive back from it. If we analyze further, we realize that abundance is our divine right. We are not separate from the source. Normally, what belongs to your parents, you inherit. It's the same for abundance and prosperity. Just take a look to the magnificent creation of the Great Spirit. Don't you see abundance everywhere? Don't you perceive the magnificence of the seas, the mountains, the trees, the rivers, the sky, the animals, and the human beings? You also have the seed of creation within you, so you have the ability to create abundance using the right tool: your mind

The angels help us to work with your mind tools and create what you deserve in life. It happens that sometimes, probably most of the times, you are saying no to the Great Spirit. Because probably you feel you do not deserve it. Probably, you feel guilty to have more than others—more than your parents, more than your family. Probably, because you have limiting beliefs regarding money.

So, what happens when we want to materialize our money goals, and nothing arises?

We set intentions, do affirmations, but still, we don't manifest it. Have you asked yourself if you feel worthy to receive? Are you a person that is always giving, but it's difficult for you to receive, even compliments? How was your family background regarding concepts and values about money?

Angels can help us to work with our mind and our thoughts that are the most important pieces regarding prosperity.

The Law of Attraction is one of the better-known Universal laws; which can help you work on manifesting your true wishes regarding abundance. The main principle is that we elaborate and create our own realities. This concept is very powerful, because you attract what you want and also what you do not want. Simply you attract what you focus on. That's why it's crucial to pay attention to your thoughts and your feelings. The three components of the law of attraction are:

1) Ask - You must know what you want. The Universe can't deliver without first knowing what you want to manifest in your life.
2) Believe - You need believe your wish will be yours. Doubts and fears just push away your work on manifesting your dreams.
3) Receive - Open your arms to the bounty of the Universe and receiving abundance. This element will be key to generate more of what you are creating.

You can practice peace with money with little exercises that will align your energy with abundance:

- Take a bill (1 or 5$, you will not use this bill anymore) and write, 'I love you' or 'Thank you.' Take this bill out of your wallet and put it in a place you go every day like your kitchen or bathroom. It will help you to establish harmony on your relationship with money.
- Take a bill in your hands, and while listening to relaxing music; start meditating on your feelings regarding money. What thoughts arise? What feelings come first? Do you hear mom or dad

complaining about money? This exercise will give you resources to work on harmony with money.

What angels say about money

When one becomes aware of the presence of God, the Divine Creator, we know we are part of this divine and perfect plan. We know that we are all children of God, and we also know that one part of divinity is within us. We know that life is full of abundance, and we are part of life. By consequence we are abundant in many aspects. We understand trees are abundant in fruits. We are part of the creation as well and can create fruits and experience abundance.

There is nothing wrong to ask the angels for our material needs. We understand that sharing and helping others is part of the chain. The angels are here to support you in all areas of your life and of course with prosperity matters. They can advise you or whisper subtle messages, such as, when you are afraid of lack of money, when you are afraid of losing your job.

The angels say that we have cascades of abundance in our interior. If we do not use that wealth; it is because we think that only that which is outside of us is valuable. The angels recommend nourishing ourselves with our own happiness—without demanding what we have or what we want others to give us.

It's very important to understand that abundance blessed by the Creator comes from your heart and not your greed. You, as anyone in this planet, deserve to experience abundance. All of us have it in some way. You may be a millionaire in laughs, in enjoying life, in having friends, enjoying your family, excellent health; for example. There are many things that do not have a price. Think of those and how rich they make you feel.

Do not be afraid to open your arms and receive abundance.. Everyone has the same right to be abundant. Allow yourself to feel in that way and open yourself to receive the gifts from the Creator.

Angels of Abundance

The Angels of Abundance will help you to create opportunities to attract more abundance in your life. They want you to be prosperous and financially free. Of course, this is teamwork; like every topic worked with angels. It's very important on this prosperity journey that your commitment and your faith be full, to be successful.

With the help of Angels of Abundance you can clear unhealthy patterns concerning prosperity and work for your goals. In addition to these angels, you can call upon archangels:

Archangel Ariel

Ariel is in charge of supervising prosperity matters. He will advise you when you need to open the roads to find wealth opportunities in all areas of your life. Archangel Ariel helps you when you need assistance for looking for a job aligned to your energy, for entrepreneurs starting a business, or when you just need help with abundance in your life. He will help you to attune with the divine prosperity, so you can open your arms to receive abundance from any source sent by the Creator.

Archangel Chamuel

This lovely archangel assists you when you need to gain self-confidence to reach your work goals. He also helps you to find lost objects, including your life purpose. He will advise you to have illuminating ideas to find the way to attract abundance in your life.

Archangel Haniel

This archangel will support you to heal any trauma that is blocking you from receiving abundance. She will help you to connect with your own light and embrace the passion for what you love to do.

Archangel Jeremiel

This archangel advices you at the time when you need to take decisions related to prosperity. He will help you to be aligned with what is good for your path.

Archangel Jophiel

She is the angel of beauty and will help you to develop beautiful thoughts and harmony with the divine property. In that way, you will work directly with the law of attraction, bringing to your life what your soul deeply desires.

Archangel Metatron

He helps you to align you to Universal laws to manifest your most deep wishes regarding prosperity. It's important to understand that these wishes have to be aligned to the divine plan to materialize in this plane.

Archangel Michael

Archangel Michael is known as the angel of protection. He is an excellent supporter when you ask for courage, strength, and when you want to eliminate fears and doubts. Michael is a wonderful advisor when you are looking for a job, when you go for an interview, or when you want to work on your life purpose.

Archangel Raguel

He works in any topic related to peace and relationships. These relationships include the relationship you have with money, or with people that own money. Raguel can bring peace and harmony with money.

Archangel Raphael

The healer of the heaven can help you to heal any wrong belief system that you have with money.

Archangel Raziel

Known as the wizard of the heaven, Raziel can help you to work with your thoughts so they can be aligned to the law of attraction. Manifestation occurs when that happens, but for that, you need to clear away doubts and fears related to prosperity—even if those come from past-lives.

Archangel Sandalphon

He is the angel of music. If your life purpose is related to music, work with him. He will be an excellent partner.

Archangel Zadkiel

The angel of compassion and forgiveness will help you with emotional healing regarding prosperity. Look upon the memories about money you have in your family, your culture, the society in which you grew up, your school. Everything counts to heal and attune yourself with prosperity and abundance.

Prayers for the Angels of Abundance

Here are some examples of prayers for the Angels of Abundance.

"Wise celestial helpers, you are the messengers of the Creator and know the gifts of the Universe. You know completely my deepest wishes regarding abundance and prosperity. You also know my life purpose and my soul path. Please teach me what I need to do to be aligned with what is for me on the Divine Plan. Please help me to open my eyes so I can identify opportunities sent for me on my abundance path. Please, support me to appreciate and be grateful for all the gifts that the Creator sends me every day. Please help me to see the little miracles, the big miracles that occur every day in my life, so I can believe that I deserve abundance."

"Angels of Abundance, please help me to clear any fear and doubt related to prosperity blocking the divine path that is sent for me. Help me to feel worthy of all the gifts of the Creator. Support me to open my arms and allow myself to receive from others, even from those I do not know. Help me to trust in the infinite and prosperous Universe and our mother Earth."

"Angels of Abundance, please help me to stay positive so I can feel in my heart, healthy emotions completely attuned to my deepest prosperity desires. Help me to manifest those desires on this plane. Help me to become a magnet of attraction and attract what is my pure heart."

"Angels of Abundance, I surrender to you and the Creator knowing that everything is already good and aligned with the Divine Plan for everyone in this Universe. Thank you, thank you, thank you…"

A Soul's Contract for a More Abundant Life

To work on more formal way with the angels, you can establish a soul contract to create an abundant life. Everything carries the power of manifestation. Try it to be realistic on your wishes and get realizable goals. This is a model proposed by Jan Kucker:

Dear God, Spirit and Angels,

This contract is to advise you that I _____ (fill in with your name) have more than completed my karmic debt, and my family lineage has completed its karmic debt, of financial scarcity and, therefore, all former contracts, karmic and otherwise, are hereby dissolved, forgiven and released by the Universal law of love and light, beginning today. Any and all poverty consciousness is healed in me, from this day forward. My soul and the souls of my family lineage are now and forever more FREED and RELEASED from a life of depravation and a mindset of limited resources.

Abundance is my birthright as is freedom of spirit, body, mind and heart. I hereby declare to the universe that I am free to enjoy abundance, fulfillment, love and prosperity in all aspects of my life, personal, business and spiritual.

From this day forward, I willingly and gratefully open my heart to receiving life's bounty and I embrace a perspective of wealth and plentifulness. My finances—bank accounts, savings accounts, retirement accounts—and my life will reflect this change, a move from shortage to joy-filled surplus.

It is my divine right to live a marvelous, rewarding life, I am declaring to the universal beings that my heart and mind are now open and receptive. I shall gratefully receive and accept all the glorious bounty and joy-filled monetary surprises the universe wishes to lovingly bestow upon me. From this day forward, I shall allow myself to attract financial rewards, relish the ease and effortlessness of having plenty and be grateful for the gifts that come as each day unfolds.

My   work   as   a
_____

(fill in your occupation) is and will always be rewarding and I through it I will help people, make the world a better place and help spread love and kindness. My work is and will always be rewarding, involving healing of the heart and soul for those who need assistance and are ready for it. My work allows me to help and show people how to live a happier life, loving themselves more each day. My work will always be filled with great joy, love, laughter and healing for me, my family and my clients. It is my divine right to be paid well for the work I do, and my finances reflect it.

I create love and loving energy all around me and it grows stronger day by day, hour by hour, minute by minute. Thank you, dear universe, angels and spirit for all of the delightful gifts I receive from you. I am sincerely and eternally grateful.

All of these requests I ask are for the greatest and highest good for myself and everyone connected with me and the work I do.

With much heartfelt love and gratitude,

_____ (sign your name)

Today's Date: _____

Some tips for manifesting Abundance

1. Ask for help

Here is a sample of a prayer you can say:

"Dear God and angels, I need help with _____ (express specifically your abundance issue). I have been dealing with it for _____ (days, months, years). I recognize I feel _____ (express how you feel.) I need your assistance to finish this cycle and embrace a new one which is full of abundance and prosperity in all areas of my life. Thank you for all your blessings."

2. Be aware of your own fears and doubts regarding money and abundance

- Ask yourself if you feel you don't deserve to receive
- Ask yourself if you are asking for something wrong. Sometimes we focus on our fears, and a thought is a prayer, so we pray for the

wrong thing.

- Feeling selfish if you ask. Sometimes you can feel your friends or family needs more than you do, and you are afraid to ask for prosperity.
- It can happen that you do not believe on angel assistance. Remember that hope and faith are the essential keys for any work on the spiritual realm. If that it's the case, ask for strength to Archangel Michael:

"Archangel Michael, please help me to find strength in my heart so I can open myself to any opportunity for my soul path and human path. Help me to get rid of any doubt and fear. Help me to overcome my own obstacles, so I can be free to embrace the gifts from the Creator and the Universe, Thank you, thank you, thank you."

3. Be grateful

Gratitude aligns us to the higher frequency of the divine realms. Gratitude also aligns you the Infinite Universal Abundance that is available for anyone in this plane. Be grateful and get ready to be on the frequency of prosperity.

4. Release past-lives vows

As explained in the chapter 'Healing with the Angels,' you can bring some imprints of vows from past lives. If you feel, that no matter you do, you do not attract abundance; then please go to that chapter and do the exercise of healing past lives vows.

5. Extra tips, some of them inspired by Dr. Doreen Virtue:

- Write, 'THANK YOU' on every check you write.
- Just trust. Let the Creator, and your celestial helpers do their job. Your job is to keep on faith!
- Repeat and repeat: I DESERVE IT. You need to believe it to attract it.
- Repeat: There is infinite supply for everyone. There is plenty of abundance for all. And there is plenty of abundance for me.
- Remind yourself: You are valuable. Money's worth is your time. No matter what someone has told you, you are valuable. You matter, and you are needed! You deserve respect.
- No fighting or chasing. What you resist, persists. If you find yourself fighting to achieve to the end of the month, start to repeat

yourself: "Abundance is my divine right. I create different forms of prosperity in my life. I attract abundance in many ways and sources."

- Economy has nothing to do with you. You are a child of good with the same right of others.
- Don't worry about competition. There is plenty for you and everyone, only you have unique gifts that cannot be compare to anyone else. Find those unique gifts!
- Clear jealous energy. If you understand there is enough for all of us, jealousy will never touch your door. Because you believe that there is a divine plan with every single human being, find the beauty in every one, and you will find beauty in your own life.
- Abundance begins in the mind first. Your mind is powerful, and it's always working for you. You are the commander. Act like that!
- Co-create with God. Positive thinking is one ingredient in the recipe of manifestation.
- Pay attention to distractions such as compulsive and addictive behaviors: overeating, substance abuse, addictive internet surfing, compulsive shopping, worrying. These distractions keep you away from your goals and dreams. Be aware of them and keep close to you a Plan to put in action when they show up in your life.
- Devote at least one hour per day to focusing upon your passions, priorities, dreams and purpose.
- Take a risk and dare to dream.
- Visualize success. Visualization always holds positive, loving images that we truly want to manifest.
- Create a 'Dream board.' It helps you to track your goals. It reminds you to remain focused on what you desire.
- Always say positive affirmations: "I am a money magnet, and prosperity comes to me on different ways from different sources."
- Stay positive! Have a list of powerful positive affirmations with you and repeat them until you believe them! For example:

> It is safe for me to receive.
> I now live according to my inner guidance.
> It is safe for me to be happy.
> I enjoy and deserve peace.
> I have compassion for myself.
> I trust and listen to my feelings.
> I am loved and supported.
> It is safe for me to be successful.
> I allow myself to receive love and support.
> It is safe to be my authentic self with other people.

I have the right to change my life to mirror my higher self's visions.
I easily let go of the old when its purpose has been served.
I take excellent care of myself in all ways.
When I win, everybody wins.

- Give yourself permission to be as abundant as you want to be.
- Balance giving and receiving. Allow yourself to receive!!
- In Feng Shui, the left corner of your home as you stand looking inward from the front door is the 'money' corner of your home. Perhaps you could place an angelic statue, symbol or crystal there to remind you to keep asking and been grateful for prosperity in your life.

Angel exercises to attract abundance in your life

Take the following steps to create abundance and prosperity in your life:

Take a moment in your busy day and close your eyes. Breath in, breath out. Look into your heart for your wishes regarding abundance. Stay here as much as you need. Then open your eyes and write them down. Be specific on your demand. Do not ask for example: I would like to receive more money or be prosperous. Tell the angels how much money need to cover your needs and desires.

If you find a limiting belief, write it down. They are tools to go deeper on your inner journey.

Now continue with the exercise and create a powerful affirmation with your wishes. For example: "I am prosperous and deserve abundance from the Universe. I work on a job that is attuned with my life purpose and brings me _____ (fill in the amount) a year."

Keep this prayer on your altar and repeat it many days. You also can have a day of abundance ritual and light a candle for the angels of abundance, repeating your prayers three times.

Remember, your job is to trust, let the boss God and the angels do their job! They are doing their job. Keep believing!! Be thankful to your angels when your prayer will be answered.

Meditation for Creating Abundance

Use the following meditation to create and attract abundance in your life with the help of the Angels of Abundance and the archangels supporting your cause.

(If you desire) Light a candle or incense and play angelical music.
Write out your prayers to the angels. Share with them your desires for abundance and prosperity and be specific.

Now, close your eyes and take several very deep breaths visualizing the Universe so abundant, so expense, so vast. Imagine the beauty and the perfection of the creation.
Now arrive on planet Earth and visualize the perfection of everything that already exists in our beautiful home: Planet Earth. Visualize the oceans, the rivers, the mountains, the forest, the animals, and your beautiful family. And now visualize a powerful light coming from a human being, this is YOU. Is it perfect, right? This is God's work. You are part of this beautiful creation.

In this perfect environment, we decide to call our helpers: the Angels of Abundance and the archangels Ariel, Chamuel, Haniel, Jeremiel, Jophiel, Metatron, Michael, Raguel, Raphael, Raziel, Sandalphon and Zadkiel.
Imagine that the angels and the archangels come and surround you filling the space and your energetic field with love and faith. They want you live in abundance because they know it's your divine right.

Remember what you wrote before closing your eyes and take a moment to go inside yourself. Imagine that you have already received what you have asked for right now. How do you feel? How are you enjoying your life and with whom?

Ask the angels trusting them to achieve your goals and desires. Ask them to guide you through the steps you need in order to bring them back to your reality. Be sure they are already doing their mission and will help you to manifest your desires into your life. They want you to be prosper and be abundant. You feel you deserve it. You embrace it with all your heart. You welcome abundance in any form, from any source, in any form. It's your divine right, and you feel it, you live it.

Once you have finished, you express gratitude to all the angels and archangels for their guide and support.
Come back to the room and drink plenty of water and write down how

you feel after the session.

For better results, you can record this meditation with your voice and allow yourself just to relax while you here yourself guiding you in this exercise.

Angel Life Coach for Abundance

Angels of Abundance work as our Prosperity coaches. You can work with them, always invoking them before starting your exercises. Try to answer these questions in a peaceful environment, lighting a candle with angelic music in the background.

- What do I remember my mother saying about money?
- What do I remember my father saying about money?
- Were there any other significant adults who modeled money attitudes and behaviors?
- What was their style of spending or saving money?
- What was the energy of my parents when they would give me my allowance or lunch money?
- Did I earn money as a youth? How did that affect me?
- How were gifts handled by my family?
- What stereotypes did I hear about rich people?

CHAPTER 10: ANGELS OF LOVE

Angels are beings of pure love. They support you in any area of your life, and love is part of it. You only need to ask for help and know that they will operate in a divine way to restore balance in your life and bring love to your heart. They will help you to find a love partner that respects you and appreciates you. However, the angels will help you to learn how to love YOU first. They want you to appreciate yourself. You already have inside you what you are looking for outside. They will coach you in manners of how you can honor your life, enhancing self-love and self-esteem.

Just be sure to be open and follow their advice trusting the process. Sometimes, it can happen that the advice doesn't match what we expect. Remember, they respect a divine plan for everyone implicated on the situation. Our mission is to trust them! No relationship is wrong. We are always learning from each other. When the lesson is done, the circle will be closed remind us the richness of that experience.

The angels help us to understand that responsibility is a key aspect in any relationship. And this responsibility includes understanding the commitment we take when we enter to the sacred space of another soul. Furthermore, this must be done without violating the free will of the others. We are responsible to remain committed without getting in the way of the opportunities that may arise, so everyone can grow physically, emotionally, mentally and spiritually. We must remember that each one that touches your life has a specific task for our soul. Open to see the purpose of any relationship. The angels also remind us that we should not take the place of other people, nor try to learn the lessons for our love partner. Unconditional love means that we need to trust in the free will and wisdom of our beloved ones.

The meaning of the word 'responsibility' refers to the quality of being responsible without interfering, to be able to concentrate on giving what is needed without attachment. But, in truth, we become a mirror for the other one and the other one for us.

As told before, we cannot truly love another person if we do not love ourselves. This is one of the main bases to embrace love with a partner. Thus, we can express love, adore, appreciate and care for this magnificent Superior Being that we are with at this moment of our life on all levels of our existence. We can express love with all our heart, our soul, our mind and our strengths. However, we must understand that what we are seeing in others, and what we are receiving from them, is a projection of what it is inside of ourselves. This can be applied to the whole spectrum of all of our relationships.

John Randolph Price wrote in, 'A Spiritual Philosophy for the New World': If you say that 'nobody wants to commit to me,' what you are really saying is that you do not want to commit to yourself, and perhaps, this is because you do not feel valuable or worthy of being esteemed. The root of this undervaluation could very well be some form of guilt that is hidden in the depths of your consciousness; a sense of guilt for some past issues for which you have condemned yourself. Therefore, you feel that you must be punished.

What you are projecting on others is: "Do not approach and do not show interest on me, because I have sentenced myself to a life of separation from any loving relationship." The other person echoes your projection and acts accordingly with what you are saying.

Kenneth Wapnick, a Clinical Psychologist who lectures and writes in 'A Course in Miracles,' comment: "What obscures our awareness of the presence of love in ourselves and in our relationships is guilt. When two people continue to learn their lessons to achieve forgiveness, their guilt decreases proportionally. The less guilt there is, the greater the love we can experience."

Each of our thoughts, words and deeds, affect in one way or another, the development of our relationships. Everything we give has to come back to us. By being fully aware that we always reap what we sow, we can begin to build a right relationship: with loving thoughts, words of encouragement and constructive actions. The angels are excellent teachers to guide us to go through all the topics about creating, building, and keeping a love relationship.

Messages from the angels concerning love

The angels want you to know:

- You are always loved, even if you are not in a relationship. When you feel alone or looking for love, just ask the angels and allow them to surround you with their celestial loving support.
- You need to trust your inner wisdom and the celestial guidance. Trusting is very important when you are doing any spiritual work, including love and self-love. As mentioned before, the angels can send you signs as coins or feathers, so you can remember you are always supported by them.
- Gratitude is a virtue. The universe will reward you with the same kind of frequency. Gratitude aligns our energy to a divine vibration to attract the same in our life, including love aspect.
- Believe that everything happens in divine time and divine order. The Creator and the angels know exactly what your soul path is, and they are already working on creating situations for you and your soulmate to connect and build something together at the right time. Just be patient and let the great divine team do their job.
- Please, do not enter in any relationship just for being accompanied. Sometimes we retard the encounter with our soul mate by being afraid of loneliness.
- Before starting a relationship, it's a wonderful idea to work on self-love. Learn how to love and appreciate yourself first. We attract in others the qualities that we have with us. We are mirrors and just be sure the reflection of your mirror is based on pure love.
- Take time to learn about you, to be with you between relationships. Be sure you have completely closed a cycle with your ex-partner before you receive a new love partner. Especially offer you time for yourself to discover the beauty that resides within you. When you are in a couple, you commit your energy to the relationship and it's difficult to find time to enjoy of yourself. Dare to learn about the most wonderful person on this planet: YOU!
- When you find a love partner, be sure he or she is your friend. Be yourself and do not play a role. Just enjoy your qualities with another beautiful being.
- Respect is the key of a relationship. To get it, you have to give it. Accept the other point of view without abandoning your values.
- Communication is essential. Listen before you talk and create space where both can express in a healthy and loving way.

Angels of love

The Angels of love guide us through the process to create, build, and keep a love relationship. They are here to help, and all you have to do is call on them. They are more than happy to support your path of happiness.

Additionally, you can call these archangels for specific issues regarding love relationships:

Archangel Ariel is the archangel of strength and courage. Ask her, when you need assistance with your energy and strength to overcome challenging situations with your love partner or people affecting that relationship.

Archangel Azrael helps you to deal with grief after a breakup and helps you through the transitional phases from being in a relationship to being single. Honor this time. It's part of your process.

Archangel Chamuel who guides you to find the partner you are seeking. Chamuel is generally the archangel who is associated with loving relationships and unconditional love. He would be the one to call on when you are looking for a love partner, to bring more love into your relationships, to learn about communication, compassion, and strengthening the foundation of your relationship. He also helps you to forgive yourself and/or loved ones, so you can move forward creating the life you desire.

If you are already in a relationship, he will help you with improving and refreshing that relationship. Chamuel will always remind you that if you learn to love yourself first, it will be easier to accept and love others.

Archangel Jeremiel helps you to review your life or relationship. He's the one to call to figure out if you should stay or leave a relationship.

Archangel Michael provides guidance, protection, and strength in a relationship. Archangel Michael is the angel to call on to help with issues related to self-esteem and worthiness in love relationships. He is the angel who will help you to protect your loved ones; and also, the one who will help you to clean up some aspects that are not working in a relationship, especially fears and doubts regarding your relationship.

Archangel Raguel brings harmony and peace in your relationships. Raguel teaches you how to become friends and life partners with your love partner.

Archangel Raphael helps you to heal your heart from past relationships and actual love situation. He will work with your self-esteem issues and push you to be ready to welcome a partner with a clean and healthy heart space.

Archangel Uriel helps you to build your self-esteem and show yourself, authentically, in your relationships.

Prayers to angels regarding love

Prayer to archangel Azrael to heal the past and forgive

Archangel Azrael, please help me to heal my heart. As you know, I've experience hurt and misunderstanding from my ex-relationship(s); and I know that the only way I have to move forward is trough forgiveness and compassion. Please dear Archangel Azrael help me to find pure love in my heart so I can be able to forgive _____ (say the name(s) of the person(s) to forgive). My soul needs to release this weight and move on to be free and be happy. Thank you!

Prayer to archangel Ariel to helps us to bring harmony in our relationships

Archangel Ariel, as you know I am struggling with some issues _____ (name those issues) in my love relationship. It's my intention to overcome those challenges and embrace a harmonious and balanced relationship. As the angel of courage, please fulfill my entire being with strength to take the right actions to create the relationship I desire. Thank you for your help!

Prayer to archangel Chamuel to find love

Dear archangel Chamuel, as the angel of love, please guide my steps to find true love. Help me to remember I am love, I am worthy, I deserve to be loved. You know exactly what there is in my heart, so please help me to open my heart completely to attract the ideal love partner. These are the qualities I am looking for _____ (name the qualities you wish on a love partner.) Help me to see those qualities within me as well, so I can be a mirror to attract what I am looking for. Chamuel, please give me patience to respect the divine plan and time accorded for my soul by the Creator. Thank you, thank you, thank you!

Prayer to archangel Chamuel for an existing relationship

Archangel Chamuel, I call your celestial presence to ask for assistance in brining understanding and commitment with my love partner. Help us both to open our hearts to have a better communication. Help us to be humble and put on the other one's shoes, so we can see with a different perspective some challenging situations we are going through right now. Teach us compassion and to experience friendship between us, so we can evolve as a couple and get stronger and stronger. Thank you for your assistance.

Prayer to archangel Jeremiel to help you to review and transform your relationship

Archangel Jeremiel, I know you are the angel that transforms difficult situations into loving experiences after reviewing the lessons of them. I call on you to help me with the following situation (Share your concern and desires.) Please bring healing to me and any other being involved, so we can release any negative feelings between us. Let us be enlightened through forgiveness and compassion, so we can live with each other in harmony. Help me to decide what path I need to take in order to achieve the life I am looking for.

Prayer to archangel Michael to help us to repair a relationship

Archangel Michael please surround me with your light of protection and be at my side guiding my words and actions. Help me to fully and completely experience love with no fear or doubts. Please help me to find courage to show all the aspects of myself in my love relationship. Please give me the strength to protect myself and love myself so I can mirror my partner as he/she deserves.

Prayer to archangel Raguel to helps you to build a long-lasting friendship with your love partner

Archangel Raguel, as angels of relationships, I come today to ask you from the deepest of my heart to bless the friendship with _____ (Name the person of your beloved one.) I ask for having a lovely, supportive, friendly, mutual, and helpful relationship. I know that your support will help me to build a long-lasting friendship with my love partner. I know that we will count on each other for any situation in the future. I know that we will do it with your angelic help. Thank you, thank you, thank you!

Prayer to archangel Raphael to find your soulmate

Dear archangel Raphael, I ask upon your help for guiding me to my soul mate. Clear my path and his/her path so we can meet each other soon. Raphael, please weave the net of synchronicity to be on the same path as my soul mate, so we can live and co-create our lives together. Please help me to get rid of any blockage in my mind and my heart that is keeping me away from living this love experience. Thank you for the opportunity to love and create a lovely life with my soul companion.

Angel Life Coaching

Move toward your heart's desire: Attract or keep your soulmate

From a meditative state, work with your angels while you elaborate a wish list of what you want to attract on a love partner and what feelings you want to experience on that relationship. Remember to express everything on your list on a positive way.

Here are some ideas you may want to explore during the elaboration of your list:

- How is your love partner? How does he/she look l? Define exactly how you want him/her to look like using specific details
- How do you feel when you are together?
- What values does he or she have?
- How does your soulmate see a relationship?
- What do you care the most in a relationship? What are your values?
- How is your life after you meet him/her?
- Describe a day with your love partner

Keep your list on your angel altar and visualize what you have written as it is happening now. Express your gratitude to the angels for their work and keep on trusting. This is your only job. The angels of love will do their job! Trust!

Recommendations to attract or keep your love partner

Step One: Use affirmations

Use positives affirmations to train your mindset. Examples of affirmations for attracting a soul mate include:

- I am love and love is my divine right
- I release any pain caused in the past by my ex love partners
- I give and receive love with an opened heart
- I attract the love partner my soul is calling for
- I am love, he/she is love, we are love

Step Two: Raise your vibration

Raise your vibration with balanced and harmonious activities to mirror the energy you want to attract. Tips for raising your vibration include:

- Spending time in nature
- Meditating and praying daily
- Increase alkaline foods; alkaline foods include vegetables, whole grains, fruits, green drinks
- Play music: angels love the sound of sweet music
- Adorn your home and office with plants and flowers
- Be in service to others
- Live in gratitude
- Dance and play
- Eliminate negative speech

Step Three: Use a daily prayer

Keep working on your mindset. Besides using positive affirmations, use a daily prayer to enhance the power of your intention. You have some examples of prayers on the section: 'Prayers to angels regarding love,' in this chapter.

Step Four: Mental visualization

Visualize yourself with your soul mate (but please with no particular person in mind. Let God, the Divine Creator do his/her work). Visualize the relationship you asked on your list. Visualize harmony, balance, happiness. Visualizing will empower the vibrations of your prayers, helping you to manifest on this plane what it is on your prayers.

Step Five: Forgiveness

Forgiveness creates a shift in energy: It sets you free. Make a list of your past love relationships and be honest with yourself. Ask yourself if there is anything you need to forgive or ask for forgiveness. Work with a person a time. Honor the lessons that a person brought you to your life and be grateful for the teachings. Then forgive! It doesn't matter if the person was wrong or right. Forgiveness is a gift you do to yourself, not to others. Forgiveness liberates you from a huge weight in your heart. Dare to forgive. This is the principal key to soul healing.

CHAPTER 11: ANGELS OF PROTECTION

Guardian angels are always working on your protection. They want to prevent any incident that cause you harm on a physically, mentally, or emotionally level.

The angels of protection are led by archangel Michael and are present every moment of our lives. They work for us on many layers of protection, so we can continue evolving and working on our soul mission. They protect us on a physical and also psychic level.

Physical protection

Guardian angels are working to prevent any physical danger. When you feel danger around you, call archangel Michael and imagine his blue indigo light covering all your body as an egg shape.

Psychic protection

Everyone is energy, and we are always moving this energy in different levels. Many components play important roles to work on these levels: thoughts, feelings, acts, food, places visited, people around you, etc. Some people have low energy and sometimes can drain our energy levels. I am not referring to good or bad people. I am referring simply to energy. If you have identified someone who drains your energy, ask archangel Michael to protect your energetic field and leave just love energy on it.

Many energy workers forget the importance of protecting themselves, and many times they take the energy of their clients. Sometimes they continue doing energy work with the leftovers from others coming for energy healing and end up harming themselves or others. If you are an energy worker, protect yourself before any session. Cover the person and yourself with a protection circle asking the help of archangel Michael. Your soul will be grateful to you for this action.

The angels of protection and prayers

Archangel Michael is the head of the archangels, the one who leads the rest of the angels. His name means 'he who is like God,' and protection is his main role. He normally carries a sword and a shield. The sword helps in the spiritual world to cut any fear and doubt that is blocking us to embrace balance and happiness in our lives. The shield is to protect us from any negative energy coming from physical, mental or psychic form. If you want to be fearless and enhance your courage, call upon him. He will empower to overcome any challenge.

He is also the archangel of the third eye and very related with clairvoyance, clairaudience clairsentience and claircognizance. If you wish to work on those areas, call upon Michael visualizing a blue indigo color.

Prayer to archangel Michael

Archangel Michael, please surround my beloved ones and me with your powerful presence. Cover me with your shield, so I can be protected anytime, any moment with your blue energy. Please clear any negativity and cut any cord that is not helping me to evolve as human and soul being. Please help me and my beloved ones to find courage to overcome the lessons and challenge we are facing now. Thank you for your help!

Prayer to archangel Michael to watch over our home and belongings

Archangel Michael, please watch over our home and our belongings now and at any time. Please keep our home safe while we are here and not here. Be our eyes, be our bodies when we are absent from our home. Fill this space with protective light and allow only love come in the house. Thank you very much!

Besides the angels of protection and archangel Michael, you can call upon archangels:

Archangel Raphael's name means 'God heals,' or 'God has healed.' Raphael is the angel who protects you while you travel, even when you are in your car going from some place to another. I used to call Raphael before starting a trip. Call upon him when you embark on a new journey, short or long. He will bring safeness and protection when you are absent from home.

Prayer to archangel Raphael

Archangel Raphael, I ask for your protection during my travel. Please protect me and my beloved ones while we are absent from home. Surround us with your protective light, so we can arrive safe and return safe at home. Thank you for your help!

Archangel Ariel's name means 'lion or lioness of God.' She is the protector of Mother Earth and the environment. She also protects the water and any activity on the waters. If you feel concerned about nature and environment, call upon her to give strength and insight for this cause.

Ariel and Raphael work together when you want to help your pets. If you feel concerned about them, ask for help to both angels.

Prayer to archangel Ariel to protect Mother Nature

Archangel Ariel, I feel the need to help Mother Earth on restoring balance and harmony. Please support us as human tribe to awaken our senses and contribute with the planet taking care of it. Please dear Ariel, keep remind me we are all part of this divine plan, and what we do to us, we do to her. What we do to her, we do to us. Thank you, dear archangel!

Prayer to archangel Ariel and archangel Raphael for your pets

Archangel Ariel and Archangel Raphael, please take care of my pet _____ (name your pet.) Help her/him to recover, to feel that she/he is loved. Give her/him strength to overcome this physical condition. Give me strength to be a good companion and supporter while she/he is through this health challenging situation. Thank you both for your help!

Archangel Metatron watches over children and guides parents when the children have any issue at school, at home, with friends. If you need help on raising your children, bringing happiness and stability, call upon Metatron, he will protect them to grow up on a safe environment with stable values.

Prayer to archangel Metatron

Archangel Metatron, as angel of children, I ask you for _____ (name of your children or any children in need). Please surround him/her with your protection and safe energy. Please help him/her to overcome any challenge he/she could pass through. Help them to conserve the innocence and the beauty of their hearts. Help me to grow up as parent and be a good supporter of his/her evolution. Thank you for your help!

Archangel Azrael overlooks newborns and help them to evolve as children. If you are going to have a baby, call upon archangel Azrael to watch over your new born and cover him/her with protective energy and love.

Prayer to archangel Azrael to assist newborns

Archangel Azrael, please assist my baby _____ (name your baby) to the transition to a new step as human being. Help him/her to evolve happily, safely, healthy, and help us as parents to be there supporting this evolution. Please keep the baby protected so he/she can grow up calm and peaceful. Thank you for your help.

These archangels and angels of protection are very happy to assist in your life. We just need to call them and be sure that they will do their job. You are always accompanied by them, just feel it with your heart and your soul.

CHAPTER 12: ANGELS AND GRATITUDE

Gratitude is an essential part in spiritual growth. Gratitude is not only the virtue that makes us thank others for their gifts, but above all it is the ability to connect with the grace of the Holy Spirit. The best way to thank God for life is to live it fully, without separatism, knowing that we are complete and one with others.

Gratitude expands awareness, opening your consciousness to receive. Every thought and feeling are clearly reflected in your body and the events you attract in life.

Giving thanks is not an act of courtesy, it is a true act of magic that we can all incorporate into our lives. Gratitude aligns your vibration to the celestial realms. At this level, you align your energy to the law of attraction, so you start attracting better experiences and people that are positive on your path.

Gratitude make us conscious about the beauty inside and outside of ourselves. This mirrors the same energy attracting beauty around our lives. Our relationships are solid and grow in a positive way; our health improves; our emotional state starts to be stable, helping us to achieve a balanced and happy life.

Gratitude makes elevate our energy to higher levels where it's easy to communicate with angels and the divine team. Gratitude can change your ideas of visions attracting more positive outcomes into your life.

Positive Energy Attracts Angels

Angels and archangels are attracted by high vibrations coming from positive intentions from people on Earth planet. That's why gratitude is important as constant practice. The celestial beings operate on this positive and pure environment, feeling attracted when similar energy is calling for help in our planet.

Giving thanks strengthens your energetic field acting like a direct call to your celestial helpers. The more you practice gratitude, the more you will be able to connect and communicate with the angels.

The Energetic field is known as 'aura.' You can practice visualizing it with meditation and visualization exercises. The aura contains colors on the spectrum of the rainbow indicating the body, mind, and spiritual condition of any person. These colors change depending of energetic field state. Angels have powerful auras, and many times are painted with their halos indicating their energetic champ.

Everyone is able to sense the energy of others. We do this in an unconscious level when we met someone. At this moment we can feel attracted or reject by the other person's energy. You can say: 'there is chemistry between us.' If you practice, you can notice the aura too. Angels can sense these auras and feel attracted immediately to anyone on a high frequency.

Everyday practice gratitude and you will be working with angels right away!!!

Angels of gratitude

Angels of gratitude help us to bring consciousness to the beauty, the perfection of the divine plan, and all the blessings that are already around us. They help us to tune in with the energy of the angels, archangels and the high energy of being.

D. Loretta Standley a metaphysical teacher and holistic health consultant mentions the following angels as angels of gratitude:

Shamael

This angel inspires gratitude and thanksgiving. This angel helps us grow closer to all of God's angels. He helps to fill our heart and mind with serenity and to love life to its fullest measure.

Affirmation: I am grateful for my faith and certainty that God is and always will be.

Prayer:
"Angel of Gratitude, there are times in my life where I have prayed and asked for things more than I have given gratitude for the things I already have. Help me to always have a faithful, serene and calming spirit and to always thank God first, acknowledging that He knows what I need before I even ask."

Ooniemme

This lovely angel is responsible for bringing the glorious feeling of gratitude to us, which expands our awareness and opens us to receive further blessings.

Affirmation: I am forever grateful for the blessings I have received from God. I count my blessings every day.

Prayer:
"Angel of Gratitude, I completely forgot to express my gratitude to God or to all my celestial team. I recognize that you bring many blessings in my life. I know that you celebrate with me, my victories, my success. I commit myself to be more thankful to you and all the beauty. Today I am grateful and say thank you."

Gabriel

Archangel Gabriel reminds us of the grace and the peace that lives with the whole creation of God. He is the messenger of the heaven and brings our prayers to the Divine Creator.

Affirmation: I am grateful for everything in my life. I see grandness and beauty all around me. I am abundant in many, many ways. The Universe always provides me what I seek.

Prayer:
"Thank you for your amazing power and work in our lives. Thank you for your goodness and for your blessings over us. Thank you for bringing hope through even the toughest of times, strengthening us. Thank you for your great love and care. Thank you because you are always with us and will

never leave us. Please renew our spirits, fill us with your peace and joy. I love you, and we need you, this day and every day. I give you praise and thanks."

Law of Gratitude

If we want to transform our relationships, we need to invoke the angels and learn different experiences from them. The law of gratitude affirms that we always return to the universe the answer that in another moment had already been granted as an action. That is why nobody can give what they do not have or do not know that they have.

By understanding deeply that the infinite Providence gives us just what we need, like the birds on the sky totally trusting the power of nutrition on the Earth; in the same way we look to another person, without saying anything, but thanking him/her from within us expressing gratitude for his/her existence. With just this action, we can radiate all the light that our inner being keep; and with these actions we heal the wounds of our own soul. We are one with the Creator and the magic of creation. As consequence, abundance is within us.

Our angelic conscience is already functioning, and it is established forever in our human reality, and perhaps, from the moment of purification, so divine.
Acknowledging the beauty around you makes you grow stronger in life. It will help you to attract more beauty and positive things in your life. Gratitude is a magnet to attract what your heart deeply desires.

If you want to work this gratitude, please focus on this simple law. The more we are grateful, the more we attract blessings to our life. The more we say 'Thank you,' the more we align to the celestial and divine frequency.

Tips to practice gratitude

- Every day find little things, situations, people that make you feel grateful for.
- Give thanks for your food and the water you drink every moment you take them.
- Thank Nature for her gifts of beautiful flowers and the sunshine.
- Listen to inspiring music to uplift your spirit.
- Keep a Gratitude journal and add to it every day.
- Tell your parents, children, love partner, friends, or beloved ones that you love them, and you are grateful for their existence in your

life.
- Nurture the relationship you have. Remember a relationship is based in two people. Work on your part.
- Smile often. A smile can make the day of someone you cross on your path. Spread happiness to people around you. It's a powerful tool they might need that day.
- Watch inspiring videos or lectures that keep you positive during your day. Choose the media that will be helpful to create a happy life.
- Be kind all the time. You do not know, who will take that gift.
- Avoid destructive messages passed through the media. Remember to choose what is healthy for you.
- Call your mom and dad more often. They are the givers of your life. Honor them.
- Cook meals with love, energize the meals with the power of your heart.
- Volunteer helping others and make your heart happy.
- Gossip and criticism are distractions on your soul work. Avoid that.
- Spend time with your children focusing on the present time. These are the moments they will carry forever.
- If a negative thought arises, stop and change it immediately for a positive thought.
- When you find yourself complaining, stop your mind and insert another cassette with a positive speech. Remember you attract what you are thinking and feeling.
- Meditate with your gratitude journal. Write in it every day as a divine practice.
- Live in the present moment. Do not worry for the past or the future. This is the moment where you live. This is the moment you are creating your life.
- Say thanks to people who offer you services everyday: your children's teacher, people at the school, people at work, the cleaning person at work, the cashier at the supermarket. Use your mind and create opportunities during your day to express gratitude.
- Call your grandparents often. They will be happy to hear about you.
- Embrace the difficult lessons arriving to your life. They will teach your soul to evolve. Just trust.
- Send love to people you dislike.
- Be thankful every time you have the opportunity to challenge yourself. That means you are growing!!
- Motivate others with your positive spirit.

- Teach your beloved ones to be grateful every moment in life.
- Treat yourself to a little pampering in thanks to your body.
- Wear clothes that make you happy, attractive, and comfortable.
- Wear your favorite perfume or cologne and think of the angels.
- Last but not less: Giving thanks to your angels and archangels for their love and support. For being with you, even when you do not notice. Give thanks for this angelic friendship!

Angel Practice: Tools to put in action

Gratitude Journal

Start by centering yourself out of noise and in a peaceful environment. You can do this exercise at your home or in nature. Light a candle, burn incense, turn on angel music and start to go deeper breathing and exhaling.

Start calling the angels of gratitude to help you to create your gratitude journal. Then you start writing: I am thankful for my life! Continue listing points of gratitude.

Give thanks to your parents for your life, your children, your love partner, your family for their presence and your friends for the adventure taken together.

List the basic needing for what you are thankful, for example, food, home, roof, car (transportation), clothing, etc.

List your abilities or gifts.

List the gifts from nature and the Universe.

List ex-love partners and the lessons they brought into your life.

List things you are thankful for, for example your bike, your cd collection you love, those tools you love to paint or create art, etc. And continue adding everything for what you are grateful for.

Close this exercise with a deep breath of gratitude.

Gratitude meditation

Start by just taking couple deep breaths. Relax the body allowing the mind to let go, relaxing the eyes, the ear, the nose, the mouth, just releasing the tension of the day allowing yourself to just be open. Take another nice breath and allow the relaxation to float through the neck and the shoulders, all the way down to the fingertips and then arriving in the upper chest, the upper back breathing releasing the energy to flow. Then take another nice deep breath, letting the relaxation float down to the tummy and the low back, moving into the hips, floating it down to the thighs, into the knees, through the calves all the way down to your feet, your toes, and then you allow yourself to feel grounded to Mother Earth with her beautiful loving energy making you feel safe. Continue to allow any cares and worries to float away and now open yourself to the angelic realm into the heaven. Take a moment to start to walk to your sacred space and see your inner temple waiting for you. This place makes you feel safe and protected. You have all the elements of this planet. Feel comfortable allowing yourself to relax into a deeper level, opening up for the angels to come in and for you to move into a beautiful session with the gratitude angels.

Start to see a blue energy floating in the space surround you with the presence of the gratitude angels. You feel almost like a whisper brushing over the body and filling you with light and love as these beautiful angels appear in front of you. Feel your connection grow to a higher level, allowing their celestial light to surround you. Feel the warmth and love, their wings lifting your heart to the next level.

You perceive their presence filling your entire place with the angels of gratitude and archangel Gabriel's peaceful warm energy. As these angels float around, you begin to feel yourself wanting to be lifted up and carried into the heaven. Let your consciousness merge with your higher self, knowing that you are divine, that you are loved, you are light, you are a divine being as you connect into this beautiful energy. You feel a source of light coming straight from the divine opening into your soul. Now you've opened the bridge of divine communication, so you can speak with more gratitude, guiding your life in a whole new way. You start being more grateful for things, and you open up.

See yourself sitting in front of a gentle stream of water that flows calmly by your side. Feel the heat of the sun on your face, which penetrates you and produces a sense of happiness. You begin to feel relaxed by the sound produced by the current and to identify yourself with it. Imagine that water runs through your own body, cleanses it, purifies your mind.

The water, the sun, the sky, everything is the expression of the angels thanking you because you are alive. Identify yourself with them and give thanks to all creation for the life that flows through you, that belongs to you and to which you belong. Take a deep breath and come to your heart center with all these gratitude feelings.

Come back to the room, drink plenty of water and write down on your gratitude journal what you are grateful of.

** For better results, you can record this meditation with your voice and allow yourself just to relax while you hear yourself guiding you in this exercise.

CHAPTER 13: ANGELS AND OUR CAREER PATH

Angels are constantly helping us in every aspect of our existence. When allowing them to assist us in the professional world, the angels are a great support to help us to find the motivation to apply for a job, to express confidence in a job interview, to thrive and show our best skills and abilities in a new job assignment, to evolve and escalate to a higher position, and most importantly, to find happiness in what we do for a living.

Each workplace has a protector and guardian angel that connects to the place's energy. Once you can establish that connection, your career path and job-related situations will improve tremendously. The main guardian angel in the professional world is archangel Michael. This fearless guardian angel will guide you to prevent mistakes, misunderstandings or conflicts with colleagues, and any other challenges that may occur at your work place.

Acknowledging their presence will make you feel you are co-working with divine helpers and partners.

Connecting with your workplace Angel

Workplace angels can be welcomed by placing a large crystal, such as Celestite, Angelite or an Amethyst, in your work space as a mini altar, along with a flower or a plant. Any black stone as black Tourmaline, black Obsidian or black Onyx, that you can place on your desk or next to your computer will work as an excellent protection shield.

If you are already working or you are starting a new job, start by creating a welcoming space for the angels. This can be done in a very discrete and personal manner. You are building a sacred relationship with your celestial helpers concerning your work.

The Archangels and Angels of Career

Every profession or career has a special group of angelic helpers. Find your career in the list below and start co-working with your angels and archangels. If your career does not appear in the specific list below, please read the last part of the section to find information for general areas. Based on the list prepared by the author Cassandra Eason on the book 'Angel Magic', the helpers on the career are:

1. Accountants, auditors, tax officials, financial planners
Archangel Metatron

2. Actors, comedians, stage and film performers
Archangel Gabriel, Archangel Jophiel

3. Administrators, local government and civil service employees
Archangel Michael

4. Advertising and publicity workers, conference, wedding, and event planners
Archangel Gabriel, Archangel Jophiel

5. Anesthetists, radiographers, and occupational therapists
Archangel Azrael

6. Artists, sculptors, and graphic designers
Archangel Jophiel, Archangel Haniel

7. Astronomers, astrologers, and meteorologists
Archangel Raziel

8. Bakers, cooks, and chefs
Archangel Sandalphon

9. Beauticians and make-up artists
Archangel Jophiel

10. Builders, and construction engineers
Archangel Michael

11. Elders care takers
Archangel Raphael

12. Car mechanics, garage staff
Archangel Michael

13. Clairvoyant, mediums, all psychics
Archangel Raziel

14. Computer programmers
Archangel Michael

15. Counsellors, life coaches, social workers, and psychotherapists
Archangel Jeremiel, Archangel Azrael, Archangel Raguel

16. Dancers, choreographers
Archangel Sandalphon

17. Dieticians, nutritionists
Archangel Gabriel, Archangel Jophiel

18. Disability workers, teachers
Archangel Raphael, Archangel Metatron

19. Doctors, family practitioners, nurses, and health professionals
Archangel Raphael

20. Drivers
Archangel Michael

21. Electricians, gas workers, technological staff
Archangel Uriel

23. Environmentalists and forestry workers, carpenters
Archangel Ariel

24. Farmers and agricultural workers
Archangel Uriel, Archangel Ariel

25. Fashion, interior design, and skin care professionals
Archangel Jophiel

26. Fertility experts, midwives, obstetricians, gynecologist
Archangel Gabriel, Archangel Haniel

27. Firefighters and rescue workers
Archangel Uriel

28. Goldsmiths and all professionals in the jewelry trade market.
Archangel Uriel

29. Hairdressers
Archangel Johiel

30. Hotel and hospitality workers, including bar staff
Archangel Gabriel

31. Journalists, newspaper editors, reporters, producers
Archangel Sandalphon

32. Lawyers, solicitors, court officials, and judges
Archangel Michael

33. Massage therapists, aromatherapists, Reiki therapists
Archangel Zadkiel

34. Musicians, singers
Archangel Sandalphon

35. Opticiansm ear specialists, dentists, and dental assistants
Archangel Zadkiel

36. Pharmacists and herbalists
Archangel Raphael

37. Photographers and the printing industry
Archangel Johiel

38. Plumbers, drainage engineers, civil engineers
Archangel Ariel

39. Police, prison officers, and security guards
Archangel Michael

40. Preschool and childcare workers
Archangel Metatron

41. Priests Rabbis and all those working in spiritually focused therapy business
Archangel Metatron, Archangel Raziel

42. Psychologists, mental health workers, and psychiatrists
Archangel Metatron

43. Real-estate agents, property developers, and mortgage brokers
Archangel Zadkiel

44. Self-employed, business owners
Archangel Raphael, Archangel Ariel

45. Spiritual healers, alternative health practitioners
Archangel Raphael

46. Women's aid workers
Archangel Gabriel

You can also count on archangel Chamuel and archangel Michael for anything relating to any job, finding objects or fixing things on your daily life.

Archangel Chamuel

Archangel Chamuel's name means, 'one who Seeks the divine.' He is in touch with the mysteries of God as well as the laws of the Universe. Archangel Chamuel helps you to connect with your life purpose, to find what makes you happy and work with your inner gifts.

Call upon archangel Chamuel to help you to discover what your soul is looking for and move into a job that is aligned with your life purpose.

"Archangel Chamuel, I am grateful for all my unique gifts that I bring to this world. I ask please to fulfill my soul's mission aligning my life purpose to the job I am supposed to do. Please open the roads for me, so I can move where my soul belongs, where my gifts are needed, and where I can expand myself."

Archangel Michael

As the archangel of universal protection, archangel Michael will release any fears, doubts, blocks or struggles when you search for a job, when you go to an interview or when you go through a challenging presentation at work. Michael will spread courage and motivation when you need to use at your workplace.

Call upon archangel Michael to remove and clear away fears and doubts concerning your job or career.

"Dear Archangel Michael, I am very thankful for your presence, your guide, and your protection. I recognize that I am dealing with fears and doubts concerning my job situation (describe your job situation.) I call upon your aid to fill my entire being of courage and motivation, so I can face this new challenge in my life. Please help me to remind my unique gifts and the input I bring to the world."

General Invocation to the angels and archangels of career for finding a job

"Dear angels and archangels of career, I request your assistance with my job search. Thank you for guiding me to find the job that is in tune to my life purpose and where I can use my unique inner gifts.

Continue to give me the inner strength and confidence in my search; and clear away all fear and doubts. I see and feel the joy of having a job right now. I know that you are working to help me to achieve my work goals and have financial freedom.

I trust the perfect outcome to my job search to occur in your perfect timing and ways. And so, it is!"

Trusting is an important factor at the time of manifesting what we are asking for. The angels and archangels will do their job! You need to do yours: trust and act always flowing with the opportunities that are opening for you on your path. Open your eyes, look both sides and trust!

CHAPTER 14: ANGELS AND MOTHER EARTH

Angels and Mother Earth are very related. Our planet is a creation of the Divine Father and Mother, so are the angels, so are the other planets, and so are YOU! Angels are working in different planes to assist the evolution of our planet. Like you, this planet (as everything that lives within) has spirit, has its own energy and its own protectors and guardians as YOU do. You are inseparable from our beautiful home: planet Earth. You are part of her ecosystem. Whatever you feel, the planet and the ecosystem feel. Likewise, whatever they are feeling, you are feeling as well.

The angels help us to raise consciousness regarding our relationship with Mother Earth. You can feel it, when you walk barefoot in a park, when you immerse into the sea and feel the energy of the sea water, when you hike a mountain and when you observe the magnificence and beauty that it carries.

We can raise consciousness every day with simple actions. We can ask the angels of nature to guide us and support us on this process of re-connection.

Nature Spirits

The Planet is filled by nature spirits, that are basically higher spirits watching over Mother Earth. Nature spirits are unseen by humans and present an evolved state of intelligence. They work together but have a hierarchy depending the evolution of the being. Billions and billions of them are living energies around the oceans, the plants, the earth, the wind, the fire.

Human beings have created a society full of stress, competition, and chaos, and therefore these spirits hide from us to protect themselves. We need to understand that everything that is in our planet and beyond is ALIVE and it's our role to respect any form of life, because it's the only way we respect ourselves. When we start respecting everything around us, a relationship starts to be built, and a connection starts to happen with these spirits. The angels of Nature can help you to connect with the spirits of Nature.

Types of Elementals and Nature Spirits

There are many kinds of elementals and nature spirits. Some of them overlook the oceans and rivers, others the mountains, others the forest, others the volcanoes. Some smaller elementals that protect the plants and flowers. In the following paragraphs, you will find a brief explanation of these elemental beings and nature spirits that live in our system.

Mother Nature

Our planet Earth is a perceptive, sensitive and conscious being. All of us live under its care like the children under the motherly womb. That is why we call the planet: Mother Earth. We take from nature everything that we need to satisfy our needs. Mother Earth gives us everything free and in an unconditional gesture of love. She is a great teacher and mother for us. She helps us to understand the meaning of connection. When we are connected to her, we are connected to all the aspects of the Universe and we understand also our role in this vast cosmos. The devas and nature spirits came from its divine consciousness, bringing with them mini characteristics of her. Planet Earth has four primary elements: fire, water, earth, and fire.

The Devas

The devas work with the angels of Nature to follow the 'Divine Plan' established by the Divine Creator. This highly evolved nature spirits work in a detailed manner, after the angels have completed their general work. They apply smoothly and with great joy what is needed for the planet evolution. Their vibration is completely different to those of humans. That's why humans cannot see them. Little children maintain their inner vibration at a higher level, and therefore they are able to see them. The main Devas are the gnomes, undines, sylphs, and salamanders.

Fire, Water, Earth and Air Elementals

These nature spirits take care of the four directions and elements of our planet. The air and fire spirit have wings, contrary to the earth and water spirits with no wings. The elementals of the fire are the salamanders; undines correspond to the water elementals; the gnomes cover the earth element; and the sylphs the air.

These higher energy beings overlook the transfer of information between the physical plane and the etheric plane, so this information can be used on the physical plane. They also help to cleanse, to clear, to transform the energy generated by the actions of human beings in our planet.

Fairies, Elves and others

Fairies are small, friendly and playful high vibration beings surrounding the plants and flowers. Children tend to see them, and many times play and talk to them.

Elves are luminous beings with a human shape. They are very small and work with magic, bringing solution for human illness. But also, they can bring illness when trying to protect themselves.

Archangel Uriel, the angel of the Earth

Archangel Uriel is the angel of the Earth and the ancestral memory kept on our planet. Archangel Uriel can help you to connect or to deep your connection with mother Earth. Uriel helps us to connect and work with our ancestors, so they can transcend from our actions. If you want to call upon him, visualize a ruby colored light covering you.

Prayer to archangel Uriel to connect to Earth

Dear archangel Uriel, please help me to connect
to the North,
to the South,
to West,
to the East.

Please, bring peace through the four elements
and to the cosmic ether that everything contains.
There is peace and love for all creatures
visible and invisible

through their kingdoms
and its elements

Archangel Uriel, please help to connect with the angels of Nature, to the
spirits of the Nature, and to your Devas.
Come to us with this rooting team
We share the road.
Thank you for your love and support.

Grounding

With modern life style, it is very easy to be ungrounded and
disconnected, especially the way we live our lives today with little real
connection to the Earth. Grounding is a paramount element when we want
to connect with nature. Grounding means to connect with the essential
aspects of this planet and the physical dimension facet. When we focus our
attention in the physical facet, we are able to attune with the energy of the
third dimension of this planet. We work directly with our root chakra. And
we are able to experience the present moment and all the gifts of the
awareness that we live NOW. We are aware that we have a physical body
and that we are able to work for its greatest good.

Why is it so important to be grounded?

- It brings the awareness to the present moment and the place of
  action
- You are able to bring healing and take care of your physical body
- Helps you to take action to implement tangible changes in your life
- Helps you to get connected with your roots and ancestors
- Helps you to release and transform your own energy
- Support your soul's evolution while you allow transfer of energy to
  the upper levels
- It provides balance and stability supporting a state of emotional
  intelligence
- Helps you to accept situations as they are

If you are a healer, it is very important not only to keep your patients
grounded, but most importantly you need to keep yourself grounded.

Am I grounded or ungrounded?

If you feel more than one of the following sensations, you may consider
taking the steps to connect with the grounding process.

Dizziness	Daydreaming
Feeling clumsy	Feeling with no energy
Heart palpitations	Nose and eyes sensitive
Feeling anxious	Not feeling focused
Forgetful	Difficulty when meditating
Difficulty to concentrate	Dreaming and no materializing

How to become more grounded

Here are some things you can do to help bring you back down to earth:

Eating healthy & balanced	Drinking water
Running, jogging, or walking	Walk bare foot on the ground
Cut back on or eliminate caffeine	Nose and eyes sensitive
Burning sage	Carrying / working with crystals
Visualization roots & color red	Get a grounding crystal to keep with you
Contact with animals	Gardening

Tools to put in practice to "Ground" yourself

Visualization

Start meditating, get to a soothe and calm breathing, and visualize tree roots.

Use color to ground yourself

Colors offer powerful vibrations. When you are near of some colors with high frequency of the Earth, you feel more grounded. That is the case of red, associated with the root chakra. Red tones will help grounding your energy. Black and brown colors and stones will also help you to ground yourself. You can visualize your body covered by these colors: red, brown or black. Or even dress in these grounding colors.

Crystals

Crystals help when we want to ground ourselves. It is better to carry them inside a little bag and put them in your pants or handbag. When I am working with them, I usually carry inside by undergarment. Some examples of grounding stones are: Hematite, Smoky Quartz, Obsidian, Bloodstone, Carnelian, red Coral, Onyx, black Tourmaline, Ruby, Garnet, Pyrite, Tiger Iron, Unakite and black Opal.

Use grounding scents

Scents can be great helpers when grounding. For example: Cedar, Vetiver, Benzoin, Myrrh, Sandal wood, Cypress, Oak Moss, Patchouli oil, Rosewood, Chamomile, Elemi, and Ylang Ylang.

Use sound to stimulate your root chakra

Certain crystal bowls, metal bowls, drums specially the native ones help you to keep you ground to Earth.

A Grounding Meditation

Start by just taking couple deep breaths. Follow by relaxing the body allowing the mind to let go, relaxing the eyes, the ears, the nose, relaxing your jaw and just releasing the tension of the day, allowing yourself to just be open. Take another deep breath and allow that relaxation to float through the neck and the shoulders, all the way down to the fingertips. Then allow that feeling of relaxation to sit in the upper chest, in the upper back breathing releasing the energy to flow, then take another nice deep breath, let that relaxation float down to the tummy and the lower back, moving into the hips floating it down to the thighs, into the knees through the calves all the way down to your feet, your toes, and then let yourself feel nice and grounded to mother Earth, allowing her beautiful loving energy to help you feel safe. Any worries float away and now open yourself to the angelic realm into the heaven.

Bring your attention to your feet and start visualizing roots coming from your feet. Imagine a ruby light flushing from the bottom of your heart to the roots, and then entering to your body. You feel the warm presence of archangel Uriel and the angels of Nature welcoming to the space of planet

Earth. You feel in your heart a portal that is opening outside. Uriel and the angels open the doors and invite you to come out.

In front of you, there is a beautiful and magnificent forest full of trees, animals lining in peace together, and a river crossing by. You feel the presence of the element air and start to perceive that you are surrounded by sylphs and butterflies. You feel the wind talking on your ears bringing you messages from the upper part of the planet. There are a condor and an eagle flying together in the sky. They dance in harmony uniting the south and the north of the planet.

You continue walking and feel the presence of salamanders and fireflies playing around you. The angels are following them. They want to show you a special place. They enter into a dark cave that is fully illuminated when the higher beings enter there. You see Uriel lighting a fire in the middle, and you can perceive some images painted on the walls of the cave. You feel these images are familiar. They are showing you your lineage, your ancestors. Your great, great, great, grandparents that came before you, walking an ancient path so you can be here today. You connect with all these images. (Take the time you need.) You start to feel so much gratitude for them, for their life, for your life. You take a deep breath and the angels grab your hands to bring you outside the cave.

Outside the cave you perceive undines and little fish playing in the river. The angels bring you over there and you plunge in the water to feel the fresh and embracing energy from this element. You dance in the water. You drink water and feel how your body receives this pure and sacred element. Water penetrates into all the cells of your body bringing life wherever it arrives. The angels show you that water is life. The undines tell you that you have a mission to protect this sacred element bringing consciousness to people around you. The angels start to wash your head and your feet, purifying booth portals that connect you with heaven and Earth.

You feel fresh and start to see fairies and gnomes playing to hide themselves behind the trees. The angels invite you to play with them. You follow them and touch the trees, the plants, the rocks, the flowers. Playing and at the same time being consciousness of the realm of life that live on everything around you. You feel connected to them.

They ask you to touch the earth, and instantly you feel the beat of the bottom of the Earth becoming one with the beats of your heart. You understand you are one with Earth. You understand that our mother gives us shelter, food, and everything we need to live in our home. You understand there is no separation and that you are family with all these higher spirits, and all the humans and animals on Earth. There is no need for competition, of stress, of suffering because you can always ground yourself and remember who you are: a child of God, a child of Mother Earth.

You touch your heart as a symbol of gratitude for this voyage. Take a deep breath and come to your center with all these gratitude feelings. Come back to the room, drink plenty of water and feel joy in your heart.

*** For better results, you can record this meditation with your voice and allow yourself just to relax while you hear yourself guiding you in this exercise.*

☐

CHAPTER 15: PRAYERS AND PRACTICE (DIY)

Please use the following exercises at your own pace. Just a reminder, be sure you are in a peaceful place where you are not going to be disturbed for the next 30 to 40 minutes. Make sure your phone is off, and any alarm is off. For better results, you can record this meditation with your voice and allow yourself just to relax while you hear yourself guiding you in this exercise.

Visualization 'Meeting your Angel'

Start by just taking couple deep breaths. Start to relax your body allowing your mind to let go, relaxing your eyes, your ears, your nose, your mouth, just releasing the tension of the day. Allowing yourself to be opened, take another nice breath and allow the relaxation to float through the neck and the shoulders, all the way down to the fingertips. Allow yourself to relax your upper chest, and your upper back breathing and releasing the energy you do not need.

Take another nice deep breath and let the relaxation float down to the tummy and the lower back, moving into the hips floating it down to the thighs. This energy continues flowing into the knees through the calves, all the way down to your feet and your toes. You feel calm, relaxed and grounded to Mother Earth, allowing her beautiful loving energy to come into your body and spirit. You feel safe! All worries float away and now you open yourself to the angelic realm.

Visualize the night with a blue sky. Imagine that you are outdoors in a splendid summer night. You are observing the intense blue sky, studded with stars. Everything around you is serenity and peace, enveloped by the color of the night.

Observe the stars, look at them, and calmly search, counting at least seven. It will seem that the stars flee or disappear from your vision. Do not worry about the result. You are not competing. Use the necessary time. Now watch carefully one single star. Isolate this star from the others and see how it shines in the sky. Slowly it moves through the sky and comes down to where you are.

As it gets closer, it becomes bigger and brighter. Its light illuminates the sky. Now it becomes like a great luminous meteor. Continue observing this transformation. In the interior of this light, a figure is glimpsed. Observe it attentively while a silhouette is being drawn: it is your Angel.

Pay close attention to this luminous being. Make a mental note of each of the details. Print it well in your mind and in your heart. It is your Angel.! Smile and walk to meet your angel with outstretched hands. He/she will come to you wrapping you completely with his/her light. You will be all one with his/her light.

A contact has been established between you and your angel. Keep focus on his/her light and when you are doing this, you can communicate with your angel. You can talk to your angel. First of all, thank him/her for having answered your call. Ask for help and protection. Ask him/her to stay by your side and come back when you need help. Keep this contact alive in your mind. It will not be difficult. The sensation is so pleasant that you will hardly tend to abandon it.

Express your love and gratitude. Use the words that will come directly from your heart. Do not look for a sophisticated language. Talk to him/her as you would speak to your image reflected in a mirror. Promise him/her the assiduity of your thought and the authenticity of your love. The angel is purity as well as energy. Greet your angel with affection and gratitude and let him/her return to the blue sky, not far from you. You have never been so far away that he/she will not be able to hear your call to intervene.

Take a deep breath and come to your center with all these gratitude feelings. Come back to the room and drink plenty of water and feel joy in your heart.

Meditation 'Connect with your Guardian Angel'

Start by just taking couple deep breaths and sit comfortably in front of plants and flowers. Observe them and connect with the beauty of nature that is in front of you. Breath in and feel how this energy of beauty reaches your heart.

Start to concentrate on the plant and perceive a luminosity radiating from the plants in front of you. Take a deep breath and feel that energy. With each inspiration, fill your heart and begin to feel a sense of love that comes from your heart, going through your head and connecting with the plant that is in front of you. This feeling of love continues growing.

Full of love energy, close your eyes and imagine the starry sky around you, imagine that all the stars connect with you. Take a deep breath and feel how the love within you grows.

Feel how that energy comes out of you through all your pores and illuminates your energetic body. This energy goes to the cosmos and comes back filling you with more love. Your being is connected to the Universe, full of energy.

Visualize on your head the image of an angel. Imagine that the light that comes from the heart center of the angel is white and golden. Inspire and feel how this light covers your head and face. You will begin to feel a tingling in your crown, a warm heat that envelops you.

Inspire even more deeply and feel that light reaches your heart. Feel peace and full joy in your whole being. When you feel this, ask your angel to give you a sign of his/her love. Bring your hands to your heart as a sign of gratitude to God and your angel. Keep as much as possible the state of happiness that is in you waiting for the signal that you asked your angel. Receive this sign with love and gratitude.

Take a deep breath and come to your center with gratitude feelings. Come back to the room and drink plenty of water and feel joy in your heart.

Angel Exercise 'Open to your Angel'

Before starting, please have your notebook and your pen nearby. At the top of a blank page, write: 'Open to my Angel,' and the date of the exercise.

Start by just taking couple deep breaths. Start to relax your body allowing your mind to let go, relaxing your eyes, your ears, your nose, your mouth, just releasing the tension of the day. Allowing yourself to be opened, take another nice breath and allow the relaxation to float through the neck and the shoulders, all the way down to the fingertips. Allow yourself to relax your upper chest, and your upper back breathing and releasing the energy you do not need.

Take another nice deep breath and let the relaxation float down to the tummy and the lower back, moving into the hips floating it down to the thighs. This energy continues flowing into the knees through the calves, all the way down to your feet, and your toes. You feel calm, relaxed and grounded to Mother Earth, allowing her beautiful loving energy to come into your body and spirit. You feel safe! All worries float away and now you open yourself to the angelic realm.

Feel a sacred space opening to yourself in front of you. Feel the presence of your guardian angel getting closer to you. Imagine that your angel wraps you gently with his/her wings. While inhaling and exhaling slowly, feel or perceive the presence of your angel, covering you and hugging you. Breathe while you focus your attention on your heart. Think about a question you may want an answer. Put in your heart that question and visualize the words written there. When you feel the words in your heart, open your eyes and write the question in your notebook.

Close your eyes again. With your question in your heart and in your mind, connect with your angel. Listen in your heart and in your throat. Pay attention to any feelings that arise. Angels come to us through feelings, so that this may be the first form of contact. Allow those feelings and remain open to the words that arise.

Open your eyes again and write down the messages you've received, by words, by images or by sensations. Remember to thank your angel for his/her message. When you have finished the exercise, read what you have received. Observe the sensations that the message awakens you. It may surprise you or perhaps move you. If the words fill your eyes with tears or if you feel moved, you will know that your angel has spoken through you.

The angels present themselves to us on the way we can receive them. If you are not sure you have received anything, close your eyes again and repeat the exercise from the beginning, establishing a more powerful connection with your desire to communicate with your angel. Accept with gratitude what you receive. Do not dismiss or criticize what appears because that will close your heart, blocking communication. When you accept, you open up; when you are open, you are much more likely to receive.

Give thanks to your angel, feel gratitude in your heart, and close this exercise by drinking water.

Angel Exercise 'Make your dreams come true'

Close your eyes and start by just taking couple deep breaths. Start to relax your body allowing your mind to let go, relaxing your eyes, your ears, your nose, your mouth, just releasing the tension of the day. Allowing yourself to be opened, take another nice breath and allow the relaxation to float through the neck and the shoulders, all the way down to the fingertips. Allow yourself to relax your upper chest, and your upper back breathing and releasing the energy you do not need.

Take another nice deep breath and let the relaxation float down to the tummy and the lower back, moving into the hips floating it down to the thighs. This energy continues flowing into the knees through the calves, all the way down to your fee, and your toes. You feel calm, relaxed and grounded to Mother Earth, allowing her beautiful loving energy to come into your body and spirit. You feel safe! All worries float away and now you open yourself to the angelic realm.

Ask your angel to release any impediment, known or unknown to you, that could hinder you in achieving your goal. Ask your Angel to help you remove them, freeing them through your roots to the earth. Now, imagine your dreams and feel yourself experiencing them at this moment. Imagine that it becomes reality and notice what you feel, the clothes you wear and the reactions of anyone who may be witnessing it. By participating in at least four of your senses, you vivify your visualization and transmit the message in your physical body.

Put this image in your heart. Ask and receive for your Angel's blessing. Feel the warmth and satisfaction of having achieved what you want. Thank God and the angels for having received it. Now, radiate the image from your heart to the arms of your angel and visualize your guardian angel surrounding it with a bubble of violet light. Observe how the bubble rises, rising and rising towards the Universe. When you can no longer see the bubble, open your eyes. Put the question aside of your mind but remain open to receive any signal that indicates that it begins to materialize. Give thanks to your angels and yourself and come back to your normal activities. Remind yourself to drink water to close the exercise.

Angel Exercise 'Cleaning the interior mud'

Start by just taking couple deep breaths, you are going to start to relax your body. One way to recognize the mud or dust that dulls our light, is to look honestly identifying the schemes that cause us doubts and unhappiness. For this, let's take a moment to meditate. Please close your eyes and enter to a state of relaxation and when you are ready, you begin to go inward and connect with the color of your own light. If you do not reach a definite color, you can concentrate on your own energy center, the source of your Inner self.

You ask the angels to help us clean the dust that obscures our brightness. Our mind keeps so many thoughts that are not helping us to shine. So pay attention, and when the mind registers something that you want to eliminate, you will visualize the cleansing angels as they rub the place with a cleansing solution, and the mud fades in the Universe to be transmuted. Let's be creative, and if you record the experience in a journal, you can write it down so you can reread it from time to time and focus on the aspects your mind needs still to practice.

The Angels help us to be authentic and follow our truth. And they do it in varied ways, since they know the divine plan for us. When we move too far from the center, the angels leave subtle traces to remind us that we must return to the road and be ourselves, something that is not always easy.

When we face routine situations, we usually start behaving as if we had connected the autopilot. Self-discovery is what allows us to discover who we are and what is the automatic program that operate our lives. When we discover a scheme not helping us, we give ourselves the opportunity to apply this technique. And even when we decide to continue, the scheme changes because we are already aware of what we are doing.

The purpose of this practice is to become authentic: the thing here is that there is no trick or special key to become authentic. Authenticity evaluates what is unique about each human being. So maybe it is necessary that each one make alterations in the practices presented here to adapt them better to his/her own soul.

Authenticity comes from true self-knowledge. 'Know yourself and you will know how to live.' When we get to know each other, we know how to deliver. If we cannot deliver, we will be caught up in the obsession for ourselves and, knowing ourselves, that obsession will play tricks on us. If this happens, we reassure ourselves and ask the angels to remind us who we are, and what our mission is here.

When we are truly ourselves, we transmit a message of love that generates a positive chain reaction in the Universe. The simple act of walking along with someone on the street could change that person's life. We can offer other human beings the angelic experience without knowing it, just as we receive experiences from certain people, and we wonder if it comes from the Angels.

Sometimes when we try to send messages, the recipient does not receive them as we want; and then, when we do not even try, the message comes to him/her with great clarity. Send positive energy radiating your light, and the light of the angels will stimulate your intentions. For example, we can consciously send blessings in rays of light or angel wings to a certain person, place or group.

We can also convey the message that we want to attract to us. This request receives a natural attention when we express to the world around us who we really are. Be alert and be aware of what you transmit and remember: when you are not harassed by doubts, you have the opportunity to act with sweetness, with charm and joy. Enjoy every day and pay attention to your thoughts. Your actions and feelings depend on the seed you are planting in your mind.

Angel Exercise 'Liberation throughout the Earth'

As you practice the grounding meditation from the chapter 'Angels and Mother Earth,' and work with your chakras mentioned on the chapter 'Angels and Chakras,' you are able to continue your practice by clearing up a specific problem that corresponds to a particular energy center. For example, security problems are related to the root chakra; loving disillusions are related to the heart chakra, etc. if you are not sure which is the chakra involved, you can cover all the bases by releasing the blockage of all the centers. A faster solution is to release from the heart and then from the root chakra.

The exercise allows you to go deeper into the subtle body, so you can get to the place where these blocks are stored. You can go through all your chakras in one session or work with one you need.

To clear a blockage of a single chakra, start by grounding yourself in your root chakra. This exercise is especially effective to release fears, doubts, disappointments and feelings of little worth, ineptitude and self-criticism.

1) Relax and close your eyes. Invite your angels to be with you. Concentrate on your breath, as you send energetic breathing to your roots on the earth. When you have penetrated and are affirmed, begin to extract from your roots the energy of the earth, taking it to each of your chakras, one by one.

2) Imagine fine herbs or filaments that arise from the crown chakra, lengthening to the sky and connecting with it. Aspire the energy of the heavens by these fibers, taking them to all your chakras, one by one. Refocus on the root chakra.

3) Check if there are emotions, memories or blockages that you need to release. In that case, concentrate on each of them. Find out where they came from and ask yourself the lesson, they taught you.

4) When you are ready to release, thank the memory or blockage and what you have learned from them. Inhale deeply and exhale the blockage with force, through the mouth, with a sibilant sound. Feel how it travels through your roots to the ground, as you exhale. Repeat twice more.

5) When you are ready, take a deep breath, bring the energy of the earth to your sacral chakra and repeat steps 3 and 4. Continue to advance through the chakras, one by one to the crown, exploring and releasing.

6) Thank your angels and Mother Earth, for working with you. Pay attention to your physical body. Pay attention to your breathing. And when you're ready, open your eyes.

Take a deep breath and come to your center feeling gratitude in your heart. Come back to the room and drink plenty of water and feel joy in your heart.

Angel Exercise 'Quick cleansing and releasing exercise'

This exercise is useful when you have little time or want to release only one thing. In case of emergency, you can do it standing; but it is better to sit, with your feet well supported on the ground. It is especially suitable for releasing resistance, obstacles, fatigue and other vibrations.

Before starting, ask for help to your angels. Start the exercise:

1) Take a deep breathe with your feet firmly on the ground. On your first exhalation, send energetic breathing to your roots on the earth.

2) When you inhale again, feel in your body what you want to release. As you exhale, visualize it and feel how it is triggered by your roots, well down to earth. Continue to exhale for as long as you can, until you have exhaled all the air from your lungs.

3) When you take the next breath, bring your eyes up, as if you were looking towards the top of your head. Inhale as deeply as you can.

4) When you exhale, send the filaments from the crown of your head to the heaven, at high speed.

5) When inhaling again, visualize the sunlight from the heaven that is poured towards your crown. Let this light fill your body and flow through your roots towards the center of the earth, with your fourth exhalation.

6) Repeat the breathing cycles twice more, up to a total of three, asking your angels for help. When you have finished, thank the angels and the earth.

Take a deep breath and come to your center feeling gratitude in your heart. Come back to the room and drink plenty of water and feel joy in your heart.

Visualization 'Healing a relationship'

For this visualization you need two candles and a quiet and withdrawn environment. Be sure you have your notebook and a pen at hand, in case you want to write down what you receive.

1) Light two candles. One represents you; the other to the person whose relationship you wish to heal. When lighting the candles, say: "I call my angels to assist me in this healing exercise. I call archangel Chamuel and Raphael right now. I invoke the angel of ... (add the name of the person to assist in this healing.) I invoke the presence of all our angel helpers."

2) When both candles are lit, say: "I consecrate at this moment, this

healing and this relationship under the light." As you exhale, visualize a healing ceremony as if it also occurred in your heart.

3) Visualize the other person. Look at him/her as he/she really is; good, bad, funny, sad, as you know it.

4) When you have reviewed the many facets of the other person, ask for a message of his/her angel. Close your eyes and let that message grow.

5) Invite his/her angel to share with you and your angel what must be done to heal the relationship. Listen to the angel response and feel it too. You may receive messages of light, color or images, as well as hearing words. Stay open to the messages you receive and do not reject anything, even if it seems silly.

6) When the message vanishes, thank the angel of the other person. Then open yourself to the answers of your own angel. Question: "What should be done to heal the relationship?" Once again open yourself to receive whatever comes without judging.

7) When you have received the message from your own angel, ask your other angel helpers if there is something else you should know.

8) Thank the angels and imagine a beautiful gift that contains the messages and suggestions that you just received. Imagine delivering that gift to the other person.

Take a deep breath and come to your center feeling gratitude in your heart. Come back to the room and drink plenty of water and feel joy in your heart. Write down in your notebook what has come to you. You can review it later as a form of insight.

Visualization 'The Angelical Umbrella'

When you want your angel protects and covers you throughout the day, open your 'Angelical Umbrella.' This visualization can be used when you have a particular goal in your mind, such as a test or an important interview, and you want to stay focused and calm. Or when you need the support of a dear friend with you.

1) Facing East, extend your arms out and say: 'Stay with me, dear angel.' Close your eyes for a moment and imagine your angel standing

behind you. His/her wings start to wrap around you. Repeat this invocation facing South, West and North. Observe if in doing that, you detect a special sensation in your body or in the atmosphere.

2) When you have completed the invocation towards the four cardinal points, sit down and raise your arms, with the palm of your hands facing upwards. Imagine your angel standing at your back, holding a large umbrella with rods made of gold. Although there is no cloth covering the frame of the umbrella, the rods are connected by drops of golden light, so you are under something resembling a gigantic golden spider web, sprinkled with a celestial dew.

3) Through this network of light fall a few drops of white and golden light, which surround you and envelop you. Move your arms to feel the powerful effects of this umbrella. While you are doing it, say: 'My angel is with me.' Repeat this as many times as you wish.

4) When you get up, feel the energetic field created by that special umbrella. Imagine it suspended above you as the rest of your day goes by.

At any time, during the day, you can say: 'Dear Angel, be with me,' and visualize again the 'Angelical Umbrella.' Unlike common umbrellas, you cannot leave this one forgotten on the bus or at the movies.

Take a deep breath and come to your center feeling gratitude in your heart. Come back to the room and drink plenty of water and feel joy in your heart.

SUGGESTED READINGS

Listed here are some of the books that I have found very supportive and helpful information throughout my journey. You may find they serve you well, too.

Brown, Denise Whichello. An Illustrated Guide to Angel Therapy. New York, NY: Gramercy Books, 2001.

Browne's, Sylvia. Book of Angels. Carlsbad, CA: Hay House, 2003.

Chantel Lysette. The Angel Code: Your Interactive Guide to Angelic Communication. Woodbury, MN: Llewellyn, 2016.

Cooper, Diana. A New Light on Angels. Scotland, UK: Findhorn Press, 1996.

Cunningham, Scott. The Complete Book of Incense, Oils and Brews. St Paul, MN: Llewellyn, 2008.

Davis, Patricia. Aromatherapy: An A-Z: The Most Comprehensive Guide to Aromatherapy Ever Published. London: Random House, 2005.

Eason, Cassandra. The Illustrated Directory of Healing Crystals. London: Collins & Brown, 2003.

Guiley, Rosemary. The Encyclopedia of Saints. New York: Checkmark Books, 2001.

Hay, Louise. You Can Heal Your life. Santa Monica, CA: Hay House, 1978.

Hicks, Esther and Jerry Hicks. Ask and It Is Given: Learning to Manifest Your Desires. Santa Monica, CA: Hay House, 2005.

Johnston, Sunny Dawn. Invoking the Archangels: A Nine-Step Process to Heal Your Body, Mind, and Soul. United States: Hierophant Publishing, 2012.

Klinger-Omenka, Ursula. Reiki with Gemstones. Twin Lakes, WI: Lotus Light Publications, 1997.

Lake-Thom, Bobby. Spirits of the Earth: A Guide to Native American

Nature Symbols, Stories and Ceremonies. New York: The Penguin Group, 1997.

Lewis, James R., and Dorothy Oliver. Angels A to Z. Canton, MI: Visible Ink Press, 2002.

Lindow, John. Norse Mythology: A guide to Gods, Heroes, Rituals, and Beliefs. New York: Oxford University Press, 2001.

Myss, Caroline, PhD. Anatomy of the Spirit. New York: Three Rivers Press, 1996.

Pradervand, Pierre. The Gentle Art of Blessing: Lessons for Living Your Spirituality in Everyday Life. Fawnskin, CA: Personhood Press, 2003.

Ruiz, Don Miguel. The Four Agreement: A Practical Guide to Personal Freedom. San Rafael, CA: Amber Allen Publishing, 1997.

Taylor, Terry Lynn. Messengers of Light: The Angle's Guide to Spiritual Growth. Tiburon, CA: H.J. Kramer, 1990.

Tolle, Eckhart. The Power of Now: A Guide to Spiritual Enlightenment. Novato, CA: New World Library, 1999.

Virtue Doreen. Angel Medicine: How to Heal the Body and Mind With the Help of the Angels. Carlsbad, CA: Hay House, 2004.

Virtue Doreen. Archangels & Ascended Masters. Carlsbad, CA: Hay House, 2003.

Virtue Doreen. Sánese con los Angeles: Cómo Pueden los Angeles Ayudarlo en Todas las Areas de su Vida. Carlsbad, CA: Hay House, 1999.

Virtue Doreen and Lynette Brown. Angel Numbers: The Angels Explain the Meaning of 111, 444, and Other Numbers in your Life. Carlsbad, CA: Hay House, 2005.

Virtue Doreen and Reeves Robert. Angel Detox. Carlsbad, CA: Hay House, 2014.

ABOUT THE AUTHOR

Lila Lotus, is an angel channeler working with angels for over 15 years. She lives in Florida with her husband and son, where guides angel wisdom classes, workshops, retreats. She has guided hundreds of clients and is the creator of Soul~ution Wellbeing and Transformational Coaching. She is also the Founder and President of 'Project Pachamama,' a Non-Profit Organization helping native people and children on the Americas.

If you wish to contact the author or would like more information about this book or Lila Lotus' services, please write the author to the address detailed below. The author appreciates hearing from you and learning of how this book has helped you to transform your life.

Please contact Lila to:

email: lilalotuscoaching@gmail.com
messenger: Lila Lotus Coaching
Facebook: Lila Lotus Coaching

For further information, online classes, the Energy Healer Academy, personal sessions, soul vacations & journeys, please contact Lila or visit us:

www.lilalotuscoaching.com
www.thehealersjourneys.com